DEATH & DYING

OPPOSING VIEWPOINTS®

OTHER BOOKS OF RELATED INTEREST

OPPOSING VIEWPOINTS SERIES

Abortion
AIDS
An Aging Population
American Values
Biomedical Ethics
Constructing a Life Philosophy
The Death Penalty
Euthanasia
Health Care in America
Mental Illness
Paranormal Phenomena
Suicide

CURRENT CONTROVERSIES SERIES

The Abortion Controversy
The Disabled
Hunger
Smoking

AT ISSUE SERIES

Smoking
The Spread of AIDS

DEATH & DYING

OPPOSING

VIEWPOINTS®

David L. Bender, *Publisher*

Bruno Leone, *Executive Editor*

Brenda Stalcup, *Managing Editor*

Scott Barbour, *Senior Editor*

Paul A. Winters, *Book Editor*

OPPOSING
VIEWPOINTS®
SERIES

Greenhaven Press, Inc., San Diego, California

Cover photo: Wayazata Technology

Library of Congress Cataloging-in-Publication Data

Death and dying : opposing viewpoints / Paul A. Winters, book editor.
    p.   cm. — (Opposing viewpoints series)
  Includes bibliographical references and index.
  ISBN 1-56510-670-9 (pbk. : alk. paper). —
ISBN 1-56510-671-7 (lib. : alk. paper)
  1. Right to die. 2. Future life. 3. Bereavement. I. Winters, Paul A.,
1965–   . II. Series: Opposing viewpoints series (Unnumbered)
R726.D435 1998
174'.24—dc21
                                                            97-21804
                                                               CIP

Greenhaven Press, Inc., P.O. Box 289009
San Diego, CA 92198-9009

"CONGRESS SHALL MAKE NO LAW...ABRIDGING THE FREEDOM OF SPEECH, OR OF THE PRESS."

First Amendment to the U.S. Constitution

The basic foundation of our democracy is the First Amendment guarantee of freedom of expression. The Opposing Viewpoints Series is dedicated to the concept of this basic freedom and the idea that it is more important to practice it than to enshrine it.

CONTENTS

WHY CONSIDER OPPOSING VIEWPOINTS?

"The only way in which a human being can make some approach to knowing the whole of a subject is by hearing what can be said about it by persons of every variety of opinion and studying all modes in which it can be looked at by every character of mind. No wise man ever acquired his wisdom in any mode but this."

John Stuart Mill

In our media-intensive culture it is not difficult to find differing opinions. Thousands of newspapers and magazines and dozens of radio and television talk shows resound with differing points of view. The difficulty lies in deciding which opinion to agree with and which "experts" seem the most credible. The more inundated we become with differing opinions and claims, the more essential it is to hone critical reading and thinking skills to evaluate these ideas. Opposing Viewpoints books address this problem directly by presenting stimulating debates that can be used to enhance and teach these skills. The varied opinions contained in each book examine many different aspects of a single issue. While examining these conveniently edited opposing views, readers can develop critical thinking skills such as the ability to compare and contrast authors' credibility, facts, argumentation styles, use of persuasive techniques, and other stylistic tools. In short, the Opposing Viewpoints Series is an ideal way to attain the higher-level thinking and reading skills so essential in a culture of diverse and contradictory opinions.

In addition to providing a tool for critical thinking, Opposing Viewpoints books challenge readers to question their own strongly held opinions and assumptions. Most people form their opinions on the basis of upbringing, peer pressure, and personal, cultural, or professional bias. By reading carefully balanced opposing views, readers must directly confront new ideas as well as the opinions of those with whom they disagree. This is not to simplistically argue that everyone who reads opposing views will—or should—change his or her opinion. Instead, the series enhances readers' understanding of their own views by encouraging confrontation with opposing ideas. Careful examination of others' views can lead to the readers' understanding of the logical inconsistencies in their own opinions, perspective on why they hold an opinion, and the consideration of the possibility that their opinion requires further evaluation.

EVALUATING OTHER OPINIONS

To ensure that this type of examination occurs, Opposing Viewpoints books present all types of opinions. Prominent spokespeople on different sides of each issue as well as well-known professionals from many disciplines challenge the reader. An additional goal of the series is to provide a forum for other, less known, or even unpopular viewpoints. The opinion of an ordinary person who has had to make the decision to cut off life support from a terminally ill relative, for example, may be just as valuable and provide just as much insight as a medical ethicist's professional opinion. The editors have two additional purposes in including these less known views. One, the editors encourage readers to respect others' opinions—even when not enhanced by professional credibility. It is only by reading or listening to and objectively evaluating others' ideas that one can determine whether they are worthy of consideration. Two, the inclusion of such viewpoints encourages the important critical thinking skill of objectively evaluating an author's credentials and bias. This evaluation will illuminate an author's reasons for taking a particular stance on an issue and will aid in readers' evaluation of the author's ideas.

As series editors of the Opposing Viewpoints Series, it is our hope that these books will give readers a deeper understanding of the issues debated and an appreciation of the complexity of even seemingly simple issues when good and honest people disagree. This awareness is particularly important in a democratic society such as ours in which people enter into public debate to determine the common good. Those with whom one disagrees should not be regarded as enemies but rather as people whose views deserve careful examination and may shed light on one's own.

Thomas Jefferson once said that "difference of opinion leads to inquiry, and inquiry to truth." Jefferson, a broadly educated man, argued that "if a nation expects to be ignorant and free . . . it expects what never was and never will be." As individuals and as a nation, it is imperative that we consider the opinions of others and examine them with skill and discernment. The Opposing Viewpoints Series is intended to help readers achieve this goal.

David L. Bender & Bruno Leone,
Series Editors

Greenhaven Press anthologies primarily consist of previously published material taken from a variety of sources, including periodicals, books, scholarly journals, newspapers, government documents, and position papers from private and public organizations. These original sources are often edited for length and to ensure their accessibility for a young adult audience. The anthology editors also change the original titles of these works in order to clearly present the main thesis of each viewpoint and to explicitly indicate the opinion presented in the viewpoint. These alterations are made in consideration of both the reading and comprehension levels of a young adult audience. Every effort is made to ensure that Greenhaven Press accurately reflects the original intent of the authors included in this anthology.

INTRODUCTION

"Our society regularly looks to technology to solve perennial human problems. Such problems as suffering and death are ones that we cannot solve, however; we can only cope with them."

—Caroline Whitbeck

A February 1997 *Los Angeles Times* article tells the story of a ten-year-old girl whose death from a malignant brain tumor became the center of a bioethical controversy over how to define death and when to end life-prolonging medical treatment. The doctors who first diagnosed the tumor immediately concluded that it was terminal. They decided that it was futile to operate on the girl since the cancer would inevitably grow and spread, and they advised the girl's family that the only useful medical treatment would be painkillers to keep her as comfortable as possible while she died. But the girl's parents, who believed that it was not their daughter's time to die, wished to pursue every measure to try to keep her alive. They sought out doctors at another hospital who were willing to perform the operation to remove the tumor.

When brain surgery failed to cure the spreading cancer, however, the young girl's condition rapidly deteriorated. She soon fell into a coma and was placed on life support to provide her nutrition and hydration. As the girl's brain tumor grew, the doctors became convinced that her coma was irreversible. A few of the doctors involved in the case felt that since she was in a permanent vegetative state, they would be justified in stopping the nutrition and hydration that kept her alive. They tried to persuade the parents to discontinue life-support measures and allow the girl to die. But the family adamantly resisted this suggestion, arguing that it would amount to killing the young girl. The parents strongly felt that removing their daughter's feeding tubes would cause her to experience a painful and undignified death. They opted to continue medical treatment to prolong her life.

When the tumor finally metastasized throughout the girl's brain, all brain activity seemed to cease. Finding no blood flow to the brain, doctors declared the young girl brain-dead. Since her heart and lungs could no longer function independently, she met all the medical and legal criteria for the diagnosis. But the parents rejected the idea of brain death. They pointed out that her body was still warm and she was still assimilating food and water. With the aid of respiratory machines, they believed, she could maintain these minimal life signs and organ functions in-

12

definitely. The family insisted that life-support systems be used to keep the girl's heart and lungs working.

For more than a year after doctors had declared her brain-dead, the girl was kept on these life-support machines, necessitating round-the-clock medical care. On several occasions she required CPR or other medical attention to keep her heart and lungs going, but other organs continued to function as before. All along, doctors argued that the life-support measures should be ended, but the parents steadfastly insisted that their daughter was still alive. It was only when all signs of life finally ceased that the family acknowledged that the little girl was dead.

During the months that the little girl's status was disputed, her case became a source of controversy among bioethicists. Some asserted that disconnecting the girl's life-support systems would be unjustifiable since doing so would certainly result in the loss of whatever life she had. But others maintained that it was absurd to keep her already-dead body hooked to these machines. The contentions over this particular case mirror broader debates in the medical community over how and when to limit the use of medical technology in prolonging the life of terminally ill patients.

Some in the field of medical ethics contend that when technological means are used to extend the life of dying patients, particularly when there is no possibility of a cure or recovery, the patients suffer unnatural and horrifying deaths. Among those who hold this view is Daniel Callahan, author of the 1993 book The Troubled Dream of Life: Living with Mortality and former president of the Hastings Center, a leading bioethics research organization. He criticizes the effect that the development of life-prolonging technology has had on medical ethics, stating that it "has led us to think of death as a curable condition, or at least indefinitely postponable."

Because twentieth-century medical technology has made dramatic leaps in curing diseases, according to Callahan, many doctors and laypersons have come to mistakenly believe that all deaths could be prevented with new technological developments. This belief, he contends, has led some to wrongly conclude that withholding measures that could extend the life of dying patients is tantamount to killing them. The resulting overuse of life-support machines has caused drawn-out suffering for many terminal patients, Callahan asserts. Above all, he argues, doctors and laypersons should bear in mind that death is the natural end of life. Doctors should be as concerned about preventing technologically horrific deaths as they are about preserving life, he concludes.

Other bioethicists, however, maintain that although patients should not be made to suffer by the use of life-support measures that are futile or burdensome to them, medical professionals should always strive to preserve the lives of patients through any means available. Among those who subscribe to this position is Gilbert Meilaender, a medical ethicist who teaches in the Department of Religion at Oberlin College in Ohio. He cautions that when doctors make a decision not to use life-prolonging technology and to allow patients to die, they may be "deliberately letting people die who aren't really dying—and doing so simply because [they] think their lives aren't worth preserving."

In Meilaender's opinion, it is morally unacceptable for doctors or patients to decline medical treatment in order to achieve a hastened death in the hope of avoiding a prolonged or more painful death down the road. It is impossible for doctors to predict whether patients will suffer worse deaths if their lives are prolonged, he contends, and in some cases, such as the permanent vegetative state, it is difficult for doctors to know whether treatment is burdensome to patients. Therefore, he concludes, doctors should always presume that the lives of patients are worth preserving and, unless death is truly imminent, they should employ life-prolonging medical technology.

The dispute over when death occurs and when life-prolonging treatment becomes unwarranted is just one of many issues surrounding health care at the end of life that have arisen due to the rapid development of medical technology in the twentieth century. As a way of exploring these issues, *Death & Dying: Opposing Viewpoints* presents debates on the following questions: At What Point Can Treatment for Terminally Ill Patients Be Stopped? Do Individuals Have a Right to Die? How Can People Cope with Death? Is Death the End of Life? These chapters examine the myriad ways people view death and dying.

CHAPTER 1

AT WHAT POINT CAN TREATMENT FOR TERMINALLY ILL PATIENTS BE STOPPED?

CHAPTER PREFACE

Linda Schneider is a terminally ill northern California woman who suffers from a genetic brain disorder. Her incurable illness causes the brain to atrophy, resulting in deafness, dementia, debilitating seizures, and eventual death. She first experienced symptoms of her illness in July 1994, and during the next few months she was hospitalized three times. At the end of September that year, she suffered a severe seizure and lapsed into a coma.

Linda had previously signed an advance directive stating that she did not want medical treatment to extend her life if she had "an incurable or terminal condition and no reasonable hope of long-term recovery or survival." Accordingly, when she fell into the coma, her husband, Lee, decided that she should be allowed to die. But doctors did not consider Linda's condition to be life-threatening. They prescribed nutritional life support and a course of antibiotics to keep Linda alive.

Linda eventually awoke from the coma, but she suffered extensive brain damage. Although she is not physically disabled or confined to a bed, medical experts agree that eventually she will die from the same type of seizures she suffered before.

Lee Schneider maintains that his wife should have been allowed to die when she lapsed into a coma in 1994. He argues that her advance directive plainly showed her desire to avoid life-prolonging medical treatment and the sort of life she is now living. His view is supported by University of Minnesota bioethicist Steven Miles, who contends that people have an absolute right to refuse medical treatment and to decide when to die. He believes that the doctors were wrong to prolong Linda Schneider's life.

But Linda's doctors disagree. They contend that the measures that kept her from dying were routine, not extraordinary, treatment. They point out that two years after her coma she was still alive and was expected to live several more years. Arthur Caplan, director of the Center for Bioethics at the University of Pennsylvania, argues that the doctors were right to treat Linda Schneider. Doctors should always treat patients unless death is imminent, he maintains.

Many doctors and families face the dilemma of when to allow a patient or loved one to die. The viewpoints in the following chapter explore the question of when it is acceptable to stop treating a terminally ill patient.

| "The hallmark of life is the capacity for consciousness. When it is erased, there are only mortal remains to be disposed of."

TREATMENT SHOULD BE STOPPED ONCE HIGHER-BRAIN DEATH HAS OCCURRED

William E. Phipps

Since the early 1980s, death has been legally defined as the cessation of all brain functions. In the following viewpoint, William E. Phipps contends that this current definition of brain death is flawed because it does not take into account patients in a permanent vegetative state (PVS) whose higher-brain functions have ceased but whose brain stem continues to regulate heart and lung activity. He argues that death should instead be defined as irreversible unconsciousness so that PVS patients can be taken off life-support systems. Phipps is a professor of religion and philosophy at Davis and Elkins College in Elkins, West Virginia.

As you read, consider the following questions:

1. According to Phipps, what was Karen Quinlan's condition in the decade before she was declared dead?
2. In the author's opinion, why should anencephalic infants be defined as brain dead?
3. What factors are leading to the increase in the number of comatose patients in the United States, according to the author?

From "Defining Death: Ethical, Moral, and Legal Factors" by William E. Phipps, USA Today, January 1996; ©1996 by the Society for the Advancement of Education. Reprinted with permission of the publisher.

Public policy pertaining to the determination of death has been altered significantly over the past generation. Because of the modification and the resuscitation I received as a result, I was not declared dead when I blacked out during my sudden heart arrest. A retired physician who happened to be nearby was attending me when my hyperventilating lungs abruptly stopped. He later informed me of recalling the instruction he had received a half-century earlier. His medical school professor had said that nothing more can be done to save a patient from dying when there is ventricular fibrillation, a precise diagnosis of my heart's dysfunctionality. Fortunately for me, paramedics quickly arrived and shocked my heart with a defibrillator. When 200 joules surged into my chest, my quivering heart returned to an effective rhythm.

Before the introduction of cardiopulmonary resuscitation (CPR) and electrical devices for jump-starting a non-beating heart, an attending physician could have presumed that cardiac arrest combined with no pulse was an unambiguous sign that a patient no longer was alive. That common sense death criterion virtually had been unquestioned from the beginning of human history until the advent of artificial life-reviving and life-support technology.

ANCIENT CONCEPTIONS OF DEATH

The ancients believed that life was centered beneath the ribs. Egyptian morticians carefully preserved the heart because of a cultural assumption that physical resurrection could not occur without it providing vitality to the body. By contrast, the brain was scraped out of the cranium and discarded since they believed it served as little more than a sponge for holding mucus. Biblical writers associated the beginning of a human "soul" with inhalation and the death of that living being with the lungs' final exhalation. Aristotle, one of the first biologists, maintained that "all sanguineous animals have the supreme organ of the sense—faculties in the heart." What we call the psyche comes from *psychein*, a Greek root meaning to breathe.

Due to our religious, philosophical, and romantic heritage, the throbbing heart has been exalted by the learned and unlearned as the main organ for revealing the crucial signs of life. Generally unrecognized in earlier history was the fact that the human personality, including intellect and emotions, primarily is the product of the brain, rather than the muscle for pumping blood through the body.

During the past generation, a more sophisticated definition

of death has supplemented the cardiopulmonary standard. In the vast majority of cases, the criteria of no beat of the heart and no respiration of the lungs still are useful. However, in numerous instances, these traditional signs of death can be reversed. By the old standard, about 15% of the comatose patients now in American hospitals would be considered dead because their breathing is not spontaneous. Many of them will regain consciousness, so it is misleading to refer to them as "clinically dead." Also, patients undergoing open-heart surgery are kept alive independent of their own cardiopulmonary functioning because oxygenated blood continues to be circulated by heart-bypass pumps.

Had the emergency squad arrived 10 minutes later, my previously undamaged heart possibly still could have been restarted, but by then the neocortex of my brain might have been destroyed from lack of oxygen. After an intravenously administered "clotbuster" drug had done its work, my heart might have functioned properly without my regaining consciousness. Occasionally, the heart of a person who is permanently unconscious continues to beat spontaneously as long as food is ingested to provide the energy for receiving oxygenated blood from the lungs.

THE CASE OF KAREN QUINLAN

After my massive heart attack, my situation could have been similar to that of Karen Quinlan and others who were diagnosed as alive even though they forever were unable to be aware of themselves or their environment. For a decade, Quinlan's permanently unconscious body continued to breathe, even after the mechanical respirator was removed. Her cerebral cortex irreversibly had ceased for lack of oxygenated blood, but her brain stem gave off electroencephalogram (EEG) signals while it regulated involuntary bodily functions. She received food through a nasogastric tube and excreted wastes through another tube. Her body shriveled to about half its normal weight and curled into a rigid fetal position. Certain organs operated spontaneously, but she remained in a vegetative state for a decade, which is not unusual in cases like hers. The person Karen Quinlan had ceased to inhabit the emaciated body; she never could think or communicate again.

By current legal definition, a body in Quinlan's condition is not dead even though it has been oblivious to its environment over a protracted period of time and there is no possibility of recovery. Most states have enacted statutes in accord with the

"Uniform Determination of Death Act" that was proposed in 1981 by a Federal commission. Moving beyond the traditional no-pulse, no-breath standard, the model law defines death as the "irreversible cessation of all functions of the entire brain, including the brain stem."

The new criterion appears to shift focus from the chest to the cranial cavity, but does not discriminate among neurological functions. In effect, the modification defines death as the irreversible cessation of *spontaneous* circulatory and respiratory functions, because the brain stem provides that natural control. This whole-brain criterion has provided some clarification, but continues to overemphasize cardiopulmonary functions while disregarding functions of the higher brain.

The discussion since Quinlan's death surrounding two highly publicized court cases relative to comatose patients further points up the inadequacy of the current definition of death. In 1986, Paul Brophy became the first comatose patient in the U.S. to receive court-authorized discontinuance of tube feeding. Many months after an aneurysm burst in his brain, Brophy's wife and children came to believe that their husband and father no longer was imprisoned in his incapacitated body. The American Academy of Neurology affirmed unequivocally that "pain and suffering are attributes of consciousness, and persistent vegetative state patients like Brophy do not experience them." After the U.S. Supreme Court decided not to consider the decision of the Massachusetts Supreme Court, Brophy's intrusive feeding tube was removed.

During the several days before his breathing ceased, his non-sentient body showed no signs of being tortured by "starvation," as some claimed would happen. Regarding patients in Brophy's condition, the Council on Scientific Affairs of the American Medical Association has asserted: "Pain cannot be experienced by brains that no longer retain the neural apparatus for suffering."

THE CASE OF NANCY CRUZAN REDEFINES BRAIN DEATH

The 1990 Missouri v. Cruzan case has been the latest to attract nationwide debate. Nancy Cruzan was without pulse or breath for at least 15 minutes after an auto accident. By use of aggressive methods, rescuers were able to restore cardiopulmonary functioning, but many of her oxygen-starved brain cells were lost irretrievably. During the seven years that followed, neurologists knew that the cells in her upper brain had liquefied—cells that cannot be renewed or replaced. Although both spirit and senses

20

were absent, her brain stem still activated some involuntary muscular reflexes. Her unseeing eyes could open, and her cardiopulmonary system continued to operate without mechanical assistance. Her throat was unable to swallow, so her heart and lungs were energized by nourishment received through a tube surgically implanted in her stomach. On visiting his daughter's hospital room during this period, Cruzan's father stated, "That's not Nancy."

In a five-to-four decision, the U.S. Supreme Court upheld the Missouri Supreme Court judgment that removing Cruzan's feeding tube was not permissible. The courts disregarded the wishes Cruzan had expressed informally before her accident. She allegedly had told a friend that she would prefer to die unless "she could live at least halfway normally." The courts did not permit Cruzan's parents, who shared their daughter's wish, to serve as surrogates and decide on a course of action. The parents were forced to prolong their agony, and publicly financed caregivers were obligated to continue treatment even though everyone knew there would be no improvement. The Supreme Court did affirm that nourishment might be discontinued if a convincing case could be made that the victim had anticipated such a situation before the accident and clearly had expressed her preference to die. A Missouri court later heard further evidence that such had been affirmed, then ruled that Cruzan's body could be allowed to expire. Several days later, after the feeding tube was removed as a result of that judicial decision, Cruzan's body quit breathing.

THE COSTS OF PROLONGED DYING

The Brophy and Cruzan cases are similar to a less publicized Illinois one pertaining to a person who has been identified only by the cost of her hospital care. "The $6,000,000 woman" was unconscious continuously following a concussion sustained in 1956 at the age of 27 until her death 18 years later. Even though neurologists agreed early in the case that her chances for recovery of cognitive functions were nil, she received food and antibiotics by means of catheters, and attendants provided extensive skin care.

How can the expenditure of thousands of dollars per week per comatose patient be justified over a period of many years when there is no reasonable expectation of a return to consciousness? Because of soaring medical costs, millions of dollars can and in some cases legally are required to be spent on each case before the brain stem ceases to function. A future epitaph might read: "Became permanently unconscious in 1996 at the age of 30, but buried in 2020."

Recognition should be given to organic capabilities of the body that are separable from the mind. Legal death even does not necessarily include reproductive functions. There are cases in which pregnancies are brought to full term and healthy babies have been delivered from brain-dead mothers plugged into respirators. In one instance, a hospital attendant raped and impregnated a permanently comatose patient. It staggers the imagination to consider the possibility of a decapitated pregnant woman, by assimilating oxygen from a respirator and metabolizing food from a tube, giving natural birth to a live infant. Significant bodily activity can transpire without orchestration by the center of the nervous system.

In *Redefining Death*, philosopher Karen Gervais argues that human death should be defined as "the permanent cessation of consciousness." Accordingly, if the conscious mind no longer can function, the person is not alive, even though the heart beats and lungs breathe spontaneously. Gervais and others hold that the *sine qua non* of human life is consciousness, not a palpitating heart. Although consciousness is not considered in the current definition of death, it is an essential prerequisite to any meaningful existence. A minimal requirement for human life is to be at least occasionally conscious, for one can be aware of surroundings and self without an ability to do much reasoning. A person with conscious awareness may have little ability to communicate, create, understand, remember, and organize.

EXCEPTIONS TO THE NEW DEFINITION OF DEATH

Gervais' proposed definition needs to be modified in order to cover anencephaly, a condition defined as "a severe and uniformly fatal abnormality resulting in the congenital absence of skull, scalp, and forebrain," where there is a functioning brain stem, but no potentiality for consciousness. Anencephalic infants may survive for days while their hearts beat, eyes blink, mouths suck, and lungs breathe spontaneously. Death should be defined to include all for whom there is no possibility of consciousness, not only those in whom consciousness has ceased.

There is a sharp line between permanent unconsciousness and the condition of amnesiacs, Alzheimer patients, or others inflicted with dementia who have lost their personal histories. Consciousness does not ensure the long-term memory needed for personal identity. Nor does the death definition being defended here include those suffering from total paralysis, severe retardation, or other debilitating handicaps. A precise, unambiguous definition giving circumstances of cerebral death that can be empirically verifiable removes these people from being classified as dead.

The magnetic resonance imaging (MRI) scan clearly can reveal areas of dead brain tissue. By means of instruments such as this, neurophysiologists can distinguish the minimalist criterion of permanent unconsciousness from intermittent consciousness or semiconsciousness. They have ways of separating those with diminished cognitive functions from those who completely lack the capacity for mental awareness. By contrast, where conscious humans are involved, the issue is where to draw the line between life and death. When the quality of conscious life is weighed, euthanasia's "slippery slope" subjective judgments arise.

Several important benefits will result from a more realistic diagnosis of death. There is a critical need to reallocate limited public funds to provide treatment for the many potentially productive Americans who cannot obtain life-saving assistance because of misplaced health care prioritizing. Why should these

vise healthy people be allowed to die while irretrievably
se patients are kept alive? Even where health insurance
er their expense, scarce health care dollars are misallo-
_ when used to maintain breath in bodies that have no potentiality for consciousness. At least $10,000,000 a day probably
are spent on such hopeless cases.

An extraordinary emotional as well as financial hardship often is imposed on the family and other support groups by a permanently comatose patient. They must stand by in anguish and
frustration awaiting the inevitable outcome that may be years in
arriving. How cruel it is to prolong the agony of these caretakers
because of an unrealistic legal definition of death.

If death is defined as the destruction of the upper brain,
more body parts can be harvested from transplant donors before
they become worthless from gradual deterioration. Surgeons
would be more willing to extract organs from the permanently
comatose if they were not fearful of criminal or civil liability.
The rapidly increasing success of transplantation has resulted in
a widening gap between requests for organs and their availability. Thousands are dying annually in the U.S. while waiting on an
organ donor list.

JUDICIAL CONSIDERATIONS

In addition to economic, psychological, and medical advantages, there also is a judicial benefit. If a victim is breathing
spontaneously, but irreversibly comatose as the result of an as-
sault, a murder charge could be placed against the attacker.
There should be no legal fiction that the crime deserves a lesser
penalty than if organic functioning were destroyed completely.
Unless cerebral death is construed as legal death, a defendant
could claim that the real killer was the party who ordered tube
feeding to be discontinued.

Americans easily are deceived by appearances. To feel the soft
and warm flesh of permanently comatose victims and see them
look as though they are taking a nap causes some to believe that
the breathing body will awaken soon. Organic motions in the
chest dupe people into thinking they are viewing a living human, even though there is no cerebral activity. Other biological
processes that normally function through brain stem regulation
cause normal blood pressure and body temperature as well as
hair growth and eye dilation.

This metaphysical confusion of appearance and reality carries
over to American funeral practices. Morticians encourage mourners to think of a corpse as though it were a living person. Their

"restoration" may include providing a healthy looking tan and removing wrinkles by means of cosmetics. After the corpse is well-dressed and the effects of death are glossed over, colored lights strategically are placed to give the flesh a vital appearance. A typical announcement such as "Mr. Jones will be at the church an hour before the time of the funeral to receive friends" might be published regarding an embalmed body. Human dignity may be denigrated, rather than enhanced, by such attempts at make-believe.

Thousands of Americans currently are in a comatose condition. A few who have been so for weeks—or even months—may regain consciousness. For many, though, the loss of those qualities that distinguish humanity is permanent. No one ever has recovered after the passage of years in this condition. Due to the development of sophisticated brain scans and other medical techniques, a high degree of certainty can be arrived at early on as to when the hemispheres of the upper brain lack the potentiality for recovery.

Never in history have so many bodies in a persistent vegetative state been defined as being alive. The amount of comatose patients in the U.S. is growing constantly due to the increasing availability of resuscitative machinery. Moreover, the number in this hopeless condition is rising rapidly as a higher proportion of the population is reaching their 90s and beyond. Only a small percentage of these had the foresight to designate, while mentally competent, conditions under which they would not want to be treated. In spite of the widely distributed Living Will, few effectively have made their wishes known in writing and/or have given someone close to them the power of attorney to act as a surrogate when they were unable to make personal health care decisions.

Consciousness Is What Defines Human Life

To be a breathing body and to be a living person are categorically different, even though the former is prerequisite to the latter. Brain stem functions have been virtually unchanged over hundreds of millions of years of humans' evolutionary history. They are essentially the same in reptiles, so they lie outside what makes individuals uniquely human. Essential for being classified as a live human is some conscious interaction with one's environment, or the possibility of attaining or regaining that interaction. Unless the gray matter in the cerebrum is functioning, human life has vanished.

Efforts need to be made in all states to release hostages from inhumane clinical technocracy. The American Medical Association wisely has advised that all life supports, including tubes for hydration and feeding, may be withdrawn from patients in a persistent vegetative status. That professional group regards the sheer prolongation of cardiopulmonary activity as without medical justification. State legislatures best can support this recommendation by replacing the whole-brain definition of death with the less stringent cerebral or neocortical definition. The hallmark of life is the capacity for consciousness. When it is erased, there are only mortal remains to be disposed of. Biological life ceases with the loss of respiration and blood pressure, but personal existence concludes with the end of psychological awareness. Psychic as well as physical capabilities are needed for personhood.

| "It is certainly possible that, even with the cessation of higher-brain function, some rudimentary cognitive capacity remains as long as the brain stem . . . [is] working."

HIGHER-BRAIN DEATH MAY NOT JUSTIFY STOPPING TREATMENT

Jim Holt

In the following viewpoint, Jim Holt contends that patients in a permanent vegetative state (PVS) confound the definition of brain death. There are two definitions of brain death, he points out: whole-brain death, which is the cessation of all brain functions, and higher-brain death, which is the irreversible end of conscious brain functions. Holt argues that evidence from cases in which people have regained consciousness from comas shows that the cessation of higher-brain functions may not end all of the functions that are normally associated with consciousness. Holt is a writer in New York City.

As you read, consider the following questions:

1. According to Holt, what functions are controlled by the upper brain and by the lower brain?
2. What is the preferred method of euthanizing irreversibly comatose patients, according to the author?
3. According to the author, what two types of coma are known to be reversible?

From "Sunny Side Up" by Jim Holt, New Republic, February 21, 1994. Reprinted by permission of the New Republic; ©1994, The New Republic, Inc.

In the course of a dinner party the other night, the conversation somehow reached the intersection of necrophilia and Hollywood. Seizing the chance, I observed that *Sunset Boulevard* was the only film in history narrated by a corpse. At this several other guests sharply demurred: What about *Reversal of Fortune?* Wasn't that narrated by the corpse of Sunny von Bulow? Well, I replied, as a matter of fact, no. While Sunny did supply the voice-over in that dramatized retelling of *l'affaire von Bulow*, she was not actually dead. She was merely in an irreversible coma. There is, after all, a difference. I mean, isn't there?

THE CASE OF SUNNY VON BULOW

In 1982, you will recall, Sunny von Bulow's Danish-born socialite husband, Claus, was convicted of attempting to murder her with an insulin-loaded hypodermic needle, and was sentenced to a long prison term. Two years later the verdict was overturned, and in a retrial Mr. von Bulow was acquitted. There had been no insulin injection, his lawyers contended; rather, Sunny's coma was induced by barbiturates and alcohol, complicated by hypothermia as she lay unattended on a cold bathroom floor at Clarendon Court, the couple's great stone pile in Newport.

At the time the trials of Claus von Bulow divided the international beau monde as deeply as the Dreyfus trials divided the Third Republic. Today they are a faint memory. Few realize that more than sixteen years after she was precipitated into a coma, Mrs. von Bulow survives in her deeply oblivious state. This beautiful and storied heiress is living out her days in a slummy quarter of northern Manhattan, at Columbia-Presbyterian hospital. Though her room is not large, it offers a fabulous view of the Hudson river and the New Jersey Palisades. She is dressed daily by around-the-clock attendants who also see to her hair, make-up and nails. A small stereo, I am told, fills the room with her favorite music.

All this, one might protest, for a breathing cadaver. At no time in the last sixteen years has Sunny evinced any sign of self-awareness. She cannot respond to stimuli—sights, sounds, touch. She is artificially nourished via a food tube. Neurological experts who have examined the damage to her brain declare that her loss of consciousness is irreversible. And yet: she *is* capable of breathing on her own, with no need of a respirator. She shows sleep-wake sequences. Now and then her lips curl into a smile. Her eyes open periodically, and have been said to tear when her two children by her first marriage, Ala and Alexander Auersperg, visit.

Improbably enough, Ala and Alex's father, Prince Alfie von Auersperg, also went into a coma, shortly after Sunny did, as a result of a car accident in Austria. He remained comatose for almost a decade until his death. The children were understandably perplexed by the shared condition of their parents, in whose memory they later established the Sunny von Bulow Coma and Brain Trauma Foundation in New York. "They're neither typically alive nor dead," Ala told *Vogue* in 1988. "What are they thinking? Are they thinking anything? Where is their 'I'? Where is their soul?"

IRREVERSIBLE COMA TESTS THE DEFINITION OF DEATH

Across this nation as many as 10,000 people are at any given moment in the same state as Sunny, according to Laurence J. Schneiderman, director of the program in medical ethics at the University of California-San Diego. They are being maintained in a coma (from the Greek word for "deep sleep"), or, as doctors now put it, in a "persistent vegetative state." The causes that brought about their PVS are various: boxing injuries, dental anesthesia, strokes, car accidents, police chokeholds, heart attacks and on and on. The longest comatose survivor ever, according to the *Guinness Book of World Records*, was Elaine Esposito: she lapsed into the state after surgery in 1941 and remained that way for thirty-seven years, until her death in 1978. The most famous—at least until Sunny—was Karen Quinlan, the New Jersey "sleeping beauty" who, in the mid-70s, became the object of a protracted and much publicized legal battle when her parents tried to have her respirator turned off.

What all coma victims have in common is a severely damaged cerebral cortex. This is the "upper brain," responsible for cognition, perception, language and purposeful movement. If there is a cut-off of oxygen to the brain, it will lay waste to the cerebral hemispheres well before it damages the "lower brain," or brain stem, which controls respiration, blood pressure and the sleep-wake cycle, as well as certain involuntary reflexes. The brain stem remains largely intact in comatose patients. Thus they will occasionally yawn, chew, swallow, sigh, grimace, laugh and cry. They open their eyes and seem to glance about; on closer inspection, however, their eyeballs are seen to be moving in uncoordinated, random directions, and there is no visual input to the brain.

The comatose sorely test our intuitions about the boundary between life and death. What precisely does "death" mean? Is it primarily a biological, philosophical or religious concept? How can we tell for sure if someone has been grimly reaped? Is there some metaphysical event, analogous to the departure of the soul from the body, that marks the moment? Today the need for organ transplants gives these questions practical urgency, just as in previous centuries the danger of premature burial did. People used to harbor a very real fear that they might be declared dead and put in the ground while still alive. And the macabre eighteenth-century tales about exhumed corpses found to have clawed at the interior of the casket were not wholly fanciful: graveyard excavations reveal that nearly 2 percent of those interred before the advent of embalming in the twentieth century were buried alive. One of the first physicians to agitate for a clear index of death was the Englishman Jean-Jacques Winslow, who in 1740 proposed putrefaction as the sure sign. It is notable that Winslow himself was prematurely interred twice as a child.

BRAIN DEATH REDEFINES DEATH

Whatever death is, it ought to be permanent and irreversible. And if there is anything on which thanatologists have always agreed, it is that the state of death is characterized by the irreversible cessation of something or other. For centuries the "something" was obvious enough: breathing and heartbeat. The permanent loss of breath was held to mark the disunion of soul and body. (Both the Greek and the Latin terms for soul—"*anima*" and "*pneuma*"—mean "breath"; the etymology of "soul" itself is unknown.) But in the late 1950s new medical gadgetry began to be developed that could take over the functions of the heart and lungs. With the artificial respiration of brain-damaged patients now possible, the continuance of breathing and circulation became disjoined from the continuance of faculties linked with the soul: thought, feeling, memory, rationality. The seat of these, of course, is the brain, which is also the locus of personal identity. "I left my heart in San Francisco"—that is a conceptual possibility; "I left my brain in San Francisco"—not likely.

Clearly, the boundary between life and death would have to be redrawn, with neurological criteria taking the place of cardio-respiratory ones. Who would do it? The Catholic Church, for one, proved reluctant; in the 1958 proclamation "The Prolongation of Life," Pope Pius XII submitted that this was rather a matter for physicians to decide. A decade later, a clear concept emerged: "brain death." The 1968 Harvard Medical School Ad Hoc Committee to Examine the Definition of Brain Death defined it as a state entailing a total unawareness of external stimuli, no spontaneous breathing and a flat brain wave. "Our primary purpose," said the committee's report, "is to define irreversible coma as a new criterion of death."

This is where matters get a bit confusing. Being in a coma, even an irreversible one, turns out to be not the same thing as being brain-dead by the Harvard criteria. Comatose patients typically have "slow" brain waves, not flat ones. Moreover, unless there is substantial damage elsewhere in the body, they are always able to breathe spontaneously, without the use of ventilators. When the plug was pulled on Karen Quinlan, for instance, she surprised everyone by wheezing along on her own for more than a decade.

HIGHER-BRAIN DEATH VS. WHOLE-BRAIN DEATH

In fact, there are two different concepts of brain death: "whole-brain death," where both the cerebral cortex (upper brain) and the brain stem (lower brain) irreversibly cease to function; and "higher-brain death," where only the cerebral cortex has sustained terminal damage and the brain stem is largely intact. What the Harvard criteria were aiming at was the more conservative of these, whole-brain death. This state is tantamount to decapitation. Once the brain stem stops functioning, traditional heart-lung death invariably follows within a week or so, even with the most aggressive support of life-sustaining gadgetry. Thus it is not possible for someone to be both whole-brain dead and at the same time in a persistent coma. The whole-brain standard was endorsed in 1983 by the President's Commission for the Study of Ethical Problems in Medicine, and has since become statute law in more than thirty states. Only a few states have adopted the broader higher-brain criterion. As for the rest of the world, virtually every industrialized country has accepted the whole-brain criterion as legal death, except, weirdly, Japan.

By one interpretation of brain death, Sunny von Bulow is indisputably alive. By the other, she is presumably dead. Which standard ought we to embrace? Reflecting on this question tends to bubble the intuition. The image of a permanently comatose but still breathing human in a coffin or crematory is a distasteful one. If the breathing is spontaneous, there is no respirator to be unplugged so that the patient can be "allowed" to die before burial/cremation. She must be suffocated, or starved to death by the removal of nourishment—which, unlike a respirator, cannot be deemed an "extraordinary" means of sustaining life. This may be excused as morally inconsequential, but it is still killing. (The preferred form of euthanasia today is somewhat subtler: since the comatose patient typically must be given medication to maintain his heart rate, and since required dosage increases over time, all one needs to do is set fixed levels of such medication; death ensues even though no treatment was actually withdrawn.) When, in 1986, the American Medical Association pronounced it ethical for physicians to withdraw care from comatose patients who met the criteria of higher-brain death, there was no implication that such patients were actually dead.

On the other hand, the destruction of the higher brain is thought not only to strip the individual of all psychological attributes—to wit, of personhood—but also to entail the irreversible loss of consciousness. And it is certainly plausible to maintain, as Arthur Schopenhauer did, that "death itself consists merely in the moment that consciousness vanishes." (On second thought, this can't be *exactly* right; if Jones suffers brain death while he is asleep, his death does not date from the moment he falls asleep.) Can a life of permanent unconsciousness—where the very possibility of having experiences is irretrievably lost—really be considered a *human* life? From the subjective point of view, is it in any way distinguishable from death?

MISDIAGNOSED PVS CASES

An unusual medical study that bears on the growing debate over how to care for people at the end of life has come to a chilling conclusion: Out of 40 British patients diagnosed as being in a persistent vegetative state, 17, or 43%, were later found to be alert, aware and often able to express a simple wish.

The study, published in the July 1996 *British Medical Journal*, is one of the largest, most sustained analyses yet of severely disabled people presumed to be incapable of thinking consciously, communicating or sensing their surroundings. The report raises troubling questions about the ability of doctors to accurately arrive at such a diagnosis, which forms the medical basis for withdrawal of life support.

Terence Monmaney, *Los Angeles Times*, July 6, 1996.

Sunny von Bulow was lucky enough to inherit a fortune of about $75 million. There is plenty of money to pay for her hospital room, her around-the-clock nursing care and so forth, and her heirs are willing to see it spent in this way. When, by contrast, in one Veterans Administration hospital an irreversibly comatose patient survived ten years and ran up a bill for millions of dollars, the bill was paid with public money. Even if some small, intrinsic value were attributed to maintaining the vegetative functions of a human organism when the person formerly incarnated in it has vanished, it would hardly justify this sort of expenditure. Some go as far as to argue that such maintenance has a *negative* ethical value, inasmuch as it is an affront to human dignity, condemning the human person to what one ethicist described as "an eternity of exile," like the Flying Dutchman or the Wandering Jew.

HIGHER-BRAIN DEATH IS CHALLENGED BY REVERSIBLE COMAS

Suppose, then, we were to redefine death to mean the irreversible loss of consciousness, the (earthly) extinction of the person, as opposed to the organism. Two snags remain. First, how can we make sure the loss is in fact irreversible? Two kinds of coma are known to be reversible: those resulting from drug overdose and those caused by the lowering of the body temperature below ninety degrees. Judging the odds of reversibility in other cases can be tricky. Even with the help of external brain scans, making a diagnosis of higher-brain death (as distinct from widespread cortical damage) is scarcely infallible. People *do* snap out of comas from time to time, a fact that raises doubts about whether PVS suffices for a diagnosis of brain death.

Item. In 1984 a Long Island youth named David Gribin went into a coma after sustaining severe head injuries in a horse-riding accident, and was placed on a respirator. After a month of unconsciousness, though, he revived. Eight years later, in 1992, he became the first coma victim to complete the New York City marathon.

Item. On March 5, 1991, a High Point, North Carolina, man who had been comatose since he had been beaten with a log more than eight years earlier suddenly regained consciousness and revealed to authorities the identities of his two assailants.

Item. In 1981 Artur Lundkvist, a Swedish poet, novelist and member of the committee that awards the Nobel Prize for literature, suffered a massive heart attack while delivering a lecture on Anthony Burgess, and fell into a coma. The doctors did not expect him to regain his faculties. Two months later he woke up and related a fantastic series of visions he had had while supposedly unconscious. These were later described in his book *Journeys in Dream and Imagination* (1992). While his body was lying immobile in intensive care, Lundkvist's spirit flew over Vietnam, to an alien planet where cows produced blue milk, to a Chicago train station where doctors operated on white people to make them black. He watched green saplings emerge from between his toes, saw cubist birds and met people who were long dead.

Lundkvist's case raises a second problem with redefining death to mean higher-brain death. How extensive must the damage to the cerebral cortex be before the constituents of consciousness and personhood—faculties such as imagination, feeling and desire—are actually obliterated? Must both hemispheres be destroyed, or only one? Must all electrical activity in the higher brain cease, or only the appearance of certain characteristic brain waves correlated with conscious thought? The danger here is the slippery slope, as the dire need for transplant organs pressures doctors to be more and more liberal about declaring potential donors dead.

Because of ethical obstacles to experimenting on human brains, not a great deal is known about the neural locale of consciousness. It is certainly possible that, even with the cessation of higher-brain function, some rudimentary cognitive capacity remains as long as the brain stem and other systems deeper in the brain are working. And even if consciousness does turn out to reside exclusively in the cerebral cortex, some opponents of the higher-brain death standard refuse to concede that personal identity can be defined purely in terms of consciousness. One such, the British philosopher David Lamb, maintains that uncertainty over which mental processes are constitutive of personhood "can only be avoided by accepting the proposal that the point where loss of personhood is certain is when the brain as a whole, and hence the organism as a whole, no longer functions." And that moment, he adds, is "when the brain stem dies."

BRAIN DEATH IS A DIFFICULT STANDARD TO APPLY

In the face of these difficulties, it is tempting to adopt a thanatological agnosticism. Some maintain, for example, that death is simply the name we give to a person's condition when certain social "death behaviors" come to be considered appropriate: mourning, reading of the will, arranging for the Social Security checks to stop and so on. Perhaps, the logic goes, there is no need to impose a single standard of mortality on everyone, and each person should be allowed to choose his own, specifying it in advance. This proposal would require some minimal neurological sophistication on the part of every citizen, of course. It would require reflection on what kind of mental or biological functions constitute one's personhood; and some glancing consideration of the many unfortunate people who are short a liver or a kidney. It would require each person to contemplate his death with a cold clarity, like a mathematical theorem. What standard of death would you choose?

What standard would Sunny von Bulow have chosen? She was decisive when it came to flowers, caviar and Parisian couture, but she was also pathologically shy, and musing on the precise moment when one checks out is a rather shy-making proposition. So it remains for us to consider: On which side of the mortal brink is she frozen in time? Perhaps there is still a "guttering flame of consciousness within her ruined brain, whose fluid-bearing ventricles have by now almost entirely usurped the place of the cerebral cortex. Perhaps, utterly abstracted from empirical reality, she is having endless hallucinatory visions in which she presides over grand, glittering parties at Clarendon Court, with—or possibly without—Claus at her side. The very thought makes her opening line in *Reversal of Fortune* almost unbearably poignant: "Brain-dead—body better than ever!"

| "Tube feeding prolongs and often worsens the dying process."

NUTRITIONAL LIFE SUPPORT CAN BE WITHHELD FROM THE TERMINALLY ILL

Anne E. Fade

Anne E. Fade is the associate executive director of legal services at Choice In Dying, a right-to-die organization in New York. In the following viewpoint, she argues that because dying patients naturally eat and drink less, and because tube feeding can cause discomfort, nutritional life support should be withheld from the terminally ill unless they specifically request it. Though it is natural for the families of dying patients to want to provide food and water to comfort the dying, Fade contends, often such treatment does more harm than good. She asserts that it is both morally and legally permissible to withdraw such life support.

As you read, consider the following questions:

1. What side effects and risks of tube feeding does Fade describe?
2. According to Robert Sullivan, quoted by the author, how can tube feeding make the dying process worse?
3. In Fade's opinion, what are some of the points about tube feeding that caregivers should consider?

Deciding to stop life support for a loved one always is wrenching emotionally. For many families, the toughest decision is whether to use artificial nutrition and hydration (tube feeding) when someone is dying.

"It is very common for people near the end of life to quit eating, or at least quit eating much, and quit drinking," explains Joanne Lynn, a geriatrician and senior associate professor at Dartmouth Medical School. "The question becomes whether we should use artificial means to circumvent their stopping eating, and the answer to that question turns on whether it does them any good."

How could being fed not do good? Most people assume that it must be painful to go without food, to die from malnutrition or dehydration. However, the medical evidence contradicts this assumption. Legal aspects of refusing tube feeding must be considered as well.

The Supreme Court and leading medical organizations agree that tube feeding is a medical treatment, and patients can accept or refuse it, just as they could ventilators, surgery, or antibiotics. Before making such a decision, though, it is important to understand what tube feeding is, how it works, and what happens when it is not given to patients at the end of life.

VARIOUS METHODS OF TUBE FEEDING

Tube feeding is the provision of a chemically balanced mix of nutrients and fluids. Most commonly, a feeding tube is inserted into the stomach via the nasal passage (nasogastric or NG tube) or through the wall of the abdomen (gastrostomy tube) by means of a surgical procedure. Another type of feeding tube is inserted surgically through the abdominal wall into the small intestine (jejunostomy tube). Fluid alone can be supplied directly into a vein through an intravenous (IV) line. Nutrition and hydration may be supplied temporarily, until the person recovers adequate ability to eat and drink, or indefinitely.

When it contributes to over-all treatment goals, tube feeding can be a tremendous benefit to some patients. It can help those who are unable to swallow, eat, or drink enough food and fluid to maintain proper nutrition and hydration. For instance, short-term tube feeding often is provided to patients recovering from surgery, greatly improving the healing process. It also may be given to people with increased nutritional requirements, such as burn victims, or those who cannot swallow because of an obstructing tumor. Total parenteral nutrition, a highly sophisticated form of artificial nutrition, can be given to individuals who have serious intestinal disorders that impair the ability to digest food. In each of these examples, tube feeding is a boon that allows people to recover completely or live fairly normal lives.

PROBLEMS CAUSED BY TUBE FEEDING

However, the benefits of tube feeding are not so apparent when it is given to individuals who are near the end of life. For example, it frequently is used for individuals with serious neurological conditions, such as advanced Alzheimer's disease or severe stroke, who cannot lead ordinary lives and never will recover. To comprehend why tube feeding may not be beneficial to such patients, it is necessary to understand the important ways in which it differs from ordinary feeding. First, tube feeding is a medical procedure. Technical skill is required to insert the tube and make decisions about how much and what type of feed is given. As with any medical procedure, side effects can occur, even with skilled care. For instance, intravenous lines can allow the fluid to leak into the skin, or the insertion site may become inflamed or infected. More seriously, frail patients receiving intravenous fluids can suffer fluid overload and breathing difficulties. Other types of feeding tubes also can cause problems. Implantation through the abdominal wall can result in surgical complications and skin infection, and may traumatize and erode the lining of the nasal passage, esophagus, stomach, or intestine.

Tube feeding differs from ordinary feeding in that it does not offer the same sensory rewards and comforts that come from the taste and texture of food and liquids. Doctors and nurses, rather than patients themselves, often control when and how much will be taken by tube. Abdominal bloating, cramps, or diarrhea may occur, especially if the patient is unable to communicate that he or she is feeling full or unwell. Regurgitation is common, and the feed may be inhaled into the lungs, causing pneumonia.

With careful attention by health care providers, many side effects can be avoided or managed fairly well. Some, though, cannot be controlled easily. Confused patients may become anxious over the tube's presence and try to pull it out. This can lead to the use of mechanical restraints—tying the arms down—which often heightens patient distress. Sedatives may need to be used to prevent agitation. Restraints and sedation sometimes have a serious effect on patients' mental states and their ability to interact or perform even the smallest activities, such as changing positions in bed. In turn, these limitations may worsen the patient's underlying condition.

TUBE FEEDING PROLONGS AGONIZING DEATHS

Most people—including many medical professionals—do not realize that dying people often feel little or no hunger or thirst and will not suffer without nourishment. Recent research supports what those who care for the dying have observed—it is not always necessary to provide tube feeding. Most dying patients feel little hunger; some stop eating completely and drink less. Severe symptoms, such as pain or nausea, almost always are due to the underlying disease, not the avoidance of food and water.

TWO FACTS ABOUT ARTIFICIAL NUTRITION

What about the cessation of artificial nutrition and hydration for the PVS [persistent vegetative state] victim? Is that moral? About a decade ago, when I first began thinking about this issue, I was far more reluctant to support such cessation than I am now. Two factual discoveries changed my mind. The first was that artificial nutrition and hydration were first developed only as a temporary means of helping a person overcome a temporary inability to eat or swallow water, e.g., as part of the recovery process in the aftermath of an operation. It was only in the 1970s, after some major improvements in the tubing and techniques of nutrition and hydration, that the procedure became more widespread, eventually being used routinely with PVS victims. My second discovery was that the inability to eat, and a failing desire to eat, is itself one of the classical symptoms of a dying body. An inability to eat was not, in the past, taken as evidence that a patient was "starving" to death, but only manifesting a symptom of a dying body. The word "starving" was only recently introduced as part of the polemics about artificial nutrition and hydration.

Daniel Callahan, First Things, April 1994.

In a 1993 article in the *Journal of General Internal Medicine*, Robert Sullivan of Duke University reviewed the medical literature about patient needs for nutrition and hydration at the end of life and discovered no evidence that tube feeding is necessary. He found that a person who stops all food and fluid intake is unlikely to experience pain and warns that the administration of small amounts of food can rekindle a sense of hunger. Even the small amount of the sugar dextrose found in many IV solutions is enough to cause the patient discomfort. He concludes: ". . . It is likely that prolonged dehydration and starvation induce no pain and only limited discomfort from a dry mouth, which can be controlled. For individuals carrying an intolerable burden of illness and disability, or those who have no hope of ever again enjoying meaningful human interaction, the withdrawal of food and fluid may be considered without concern that it will add to the misery." Patients at the end of life who avoid nutrition and hydration quickly slip into a coma, a sleeplike state that inherently is free of pain. In contrast, tube feeding prolongs and often worsens the dying process.

The terminally ill sometimes can benefit temporarily from tube feeding, but to assume that it always must be provided fails to consider patient needs. Because we ourselves tend to see the provision of food and water as intrinsic to caring, we sometimes feel uncomfortable about withholding tube feeding. When we are entrusted with making decisions for the dying, we need to broaden our understanding of caring, so that we address the *patient's* comfort before our own.

As with any medical treatment, tube feeding and hydration should be given if they contribute to over-all treatment goals. These always should focus on the patient's wishes and interests. Thus, if the aim is to keep a patient alive, tube feeding may be essential. However, if the object is to provide comfort care only, tube feeding usually is not appropriate and actually may add to discomfort.

THE URGE TO PROVIDE FOOD AND WATER

The notion that dying patients must be provided with nutrition and fluids continues to be a powerful one. Lynn suggests some of the reasons for this when she notes: "Our instinct is to provide food. Feeding another person is the way of showing that you care about them, and failure to feed ordinarily is a way of showing that you *don't* care."

Normally, feeding a helpless person—a baby or an invalid, for example—is a lifesaving and deeply caring act. When someone is dying and "nothing more can be done," the desire to do *something* to show our caring often becomes acute. This urge reflects a sense of powerlessness in the face of death and may lead to actions that are not in the best interest of the patient.

Because food and water have enormous symbolic significance for most of us, it often is difficult to decide about the use of tube feeding solely on clinical criteria. It is one thing when a competent dying person refuses tube feeding and can explain the choice and reassure loved ones that he or she is not in pain. It is another to make that decision for someone who is unconscious or incompetent. These situations force families to examine carefully reasons for providing or withholding tube feeding.

Because of personal or religious conviction, some individuals may believe that nutrition and fluids always must be given, no matter what the condition or prognosis or how much the patient may be suffering. If this is consistent with the patient's beliefs, caregivers should respect his or her wishes to continue treatment. However, a family's decision to continue tube feeding may need closer examination if it will not benefit the patient and evidence is lacking that he or she would want the procedure.

The symbolism of feeding as a sign of caring can be so powerful that even families who know that their loved one would not want to be kept alive still may be unable to bring themselves to stop tube feeding. In such cases, according to Lynn and other geriatricians, a compromise often can be reached.

"Usually, you can honor the symbol without hurting the patient," she explains. "You can run an IV with the family's awareness that it's at a very low rate," so that it does not cause side effects, but the family is reassured. The moment when family members are watching a loved one die is not the time to debate their assumptions or educate them about the physiology of the dying process.

THE LEGAL RIGHT TO REFUSE TUBE FEEDING

Misunderstanding about the law may interfere with decisions to forgo tube feeding. Many health care professionals do not know that tube feeding legally may be refused at the end of life. "We receive calls from around the country every day from people with questions about end-of-life care," notes Anna Moretti, staff attorney for Choice In Dying, a nonprofit organization that serves the needs of dying patients and their families, "and the vast majority of those calls concern tube feeding." A patient who still has the capacity to make decisions can tell the physician what he or she wants. For those who are too sick to communicate, though, the rules vary from state to state.

Every state law allows individuals to refuse tube feeding through the use of an advance directive such as a living will or medical power of attorney. Both types of advance directives let you give instructions about your future medical care in the event that you become unable to speak for yourself because of a serious illness or incapacity. A living will lets you put in writing your wishes about medical treatment; a medical power of attorney lets you appoint someone you trust to make decisions about your medical care. Each state, however, has its own rules about how you must indicate your wishes about tube feeding. . . .

"Several states require individuals to state specifically in their advance directive forms whether or not they would want tube feeding at the end of life. Ohio, for instance, goes so far as to require that instructions refusing tube feeding must be printed in capital letters," explains Moretti. It is important to follow these state rules because treatment usually will be given when uncertainty or conflict exists about whether or not a person would want it. Because tube feeding is such an emotionally charged issue and caregivers' views may be very different from the patient's views, experts advise that everyone should make their wishes about its use explicit, regardless of the state rules. "It's not enough just to record your wishes in advance directives," Moretti cautions, "you also need to talk over your wishes with your loved ones so they can accept and understand the choices you have made."

MAKING TREATMENT DECISIONS WITHOUT AN ADVANCE DIRECTIVE

What happens if a patient has not completed an advance directive? Again, the answer depends on state law. While many states permit families to make decisions about life support, including tube feeding, when the patient no longer can make decisions for himself or herself, a few require families to produce proof that the patient would not want the treatment. At times, this can be difficult. Usually, it would consist of conversations about medical treatment wishes family members may have had with the patient in the past. Many people have a general sense of what their loved ones would want, but have not had the detailed conversations that would satisfy legal requirements.

If individuals have made their wishes known, either through a written advance directive or conversations with others, the physician must honor those wishes or transfer their care to another doctor who will honor them. People should talk about their wishes for end-of-life medical treatment with their physicians in advance, before a medical crisis arises. That way, agreements about treatment can be worked out ahead of time and, if the doctor seems unwilling to honor a request to forgo life support, the patient can consider finding another physician.

Some nursing homes and hospitals, for religious or other reasons, may have policies in place that would prevent them from honoring a patient's legal right to refuse medical treatment. Under the Federal Patient Self-Determination Act, health care facilities are required to tell patients at the time of admission about any policy that would prevent honoring a request to stop treatment. Facilities that have such policies generally are required to transfer a patient to one that will honor his or her wishes. Practically speaking, though, it can be very difficult to arrange a transfer to another facility for the sole purpose of honoring a patient's refusal of treatment. Therefore, it is better to find out in advance what a health care facility's policies are about requests to stop life support. If individuals can anticipate that they some day might receive treatment in a particular hospital or nursing home, or if a loved one is about to be admitted to a nursing home, they should find out the institution's policy in advance.

REFUSING TUBE FEEDING IS NOT SUICIDE

It is important to remember that refusing tube feeding is not considered suicide. A person at the end of life is dying, not by choice, but because of a particular condition or disease. Continuing treatment may delay the moment of death, but cannot alter the underlying medical condition. The person's death is considered to be due to the underlying medical condition and therefore is not deemed suicide. Similarly, life insurance policies are not affected if life-sustaining treatments, including tube feeding, are refused.

If you are the caregiver, some points to consider when making a decision about the use of tube feeding include:

• What are the patient's wishes? What quality of life is important to the patient?

• What is the goal or purpose in providing tube feeding? Will it prolong the patient's life? Will it contribute to the patient's comfort?

• Does the patient have religious, cultural, or personal values that would affect the decision to stop treatment?

• Are depression, inability to let go, guilt, unresolved issues from the past, or unfinished business affecting the decision-making process of the patient, surrogate decision-maker, or health care provider?

• Does the state law affect the decision to stop treatment?

Watching someone we love die makes us feel powerless. Even when nothing can be done to cure the disease, a great deal can be done to make the person's last days comfortable and even productive and meaningful. As we broaden our understanding of providing care to the dying, we are improving the management of pain and other symptoms. Through the exceptional work of the hospice movement, we have come to recognize that care of the dying requires medical expertise and a collaborative approach among all of the patient's caregivers. This allows them to consider the total needs of the patient. It is important to remember that, when we are entrusted with decisions about the care of the dying, the patient's comfort and wishes must guide our decision-making, not our own.

"I cannot understand taking away
food and fluid before the body itself
decides to quit."

NUTRITIONAL LIFE SUPPORT SHOULD NOT BE WITHHELD FROM THE TERMINALLY ILL

Nancy Harvey

People's unwarranted fear of a painful death unnaturally prolonged by technology prompts them to support euthanasia for dying or permanently vegetative patients, Nancy Harvey maintains in the following viewpoint. However, she argues, withholding food and water causes a much worse death than the "technological bad death" that people fear. Nutrition and hydration should always be provided to the dying, she contends. Harvey teaches French and English at Cuba High School, in Cuba, Missouri.

As you read, consider the following questions:

1. In Harvey's opinion, what are some forms of everyday technology that many people could not live without?
2. According to the author, what are some "futile" treatments that are provided for the comfort of dying patients?
3. What does the quality of a helpless person's life depend on, in the author's view?

From "Dying Like a Dog" by Nancy Harvey, First Things, April 1995; © Institute on Religion and Public Life. Reprinted by permission of the publisher.

Hunger and thirst, starvation and dehydration—ugly words to most of us, bringing images of tormenting weakness, agonizing muscle spasms, the ultimate cannibalism as the body devours itself to stay alive. But not everyone views such words with disgust. In May 1994, St. Louis University, a private Catholic school, held a conference on medical ethics that included a workshop entitled, "Dying of Dehydration—Does It Hurt?" In April 1994, some contributors to the symposium in *First Things* on medical ethics, "The Sanctity of Life Seduced," recommended starvation and dehydration for certain terminal patients and those in a "persistent vegetative state" (PVS). Living wills list artificially administered food and water as things that may be taken away, and newspaper and magazine articles continue to suggest that modern technologies for continuing food and water cause the terminally ill to suffer long and agonizing "bad deaths," or (if they are in PVS) "bad lives" without human capacities.

The people who recommend starvation and dehydration are not monsters or throwbacks to the Third Reich. They seem to be genuinely concerned with the pain and ugliness of "bad death," and some of them are worried that the horrors of technological death increase grassroots support for the euthanasia movement. Those who favor removing food and water have impressive credentials. They include lawyers, doctors, and medical ethicists. However, I wonder how many of them have experienced dehydration and starvation almost to the point of death; how many of them have spent time in the sick bed?

A Personal Account of Disability and Dehydration

I am a patient—not terminal or in PVS, but very expensive to keep alive, and more and more aware, as I grow older, of what it means to regard food and water as options instead of necessities. I have had scurvy, liver damage, compression fractures, staph infections, seizures, kidney failure, and many episodes of severe dehydration and malnutrition (one almost fatal). Having had surgery for Crohn's disease, I am kept alive by very expensive hydration and nutrition that goes directly into the bloodstream. Poor health has been a part of my life for twenty-three years.

During this time, I have not noticed that my doctors are afflicted with the hubris that regards death as an accident that can be prevented. Perhaps because they work with chronic disease, my doctors tend to have a very fatalistic attitude. They know they cannot overcome death. All they can do is buy time—and few of them want to buy time for a dying patient in great pain.

Yet ordinary people seem to have gotten the impression that

this is exactly what doctors most want to do. Ordinary people seem haunted by the nightmare of the technological "bad death." An old woman full of cancer has her heart stop. Instantly the medics rush in with the paddles to start her up again. A respirator is hooked up. Her gut shut down a couple of days ago, so she already has a central line. Her kidneys quit yesterday, and she is now on dialysis. The medics shock her heart back into action, make sure the beat is regular, check all systems, and leave, after hooking her up to a heart monitor. But late that night the nurses are called away from their stations to tend to others. There is no one watching the monitor. The woman's heart stops—this time forever.

TUBE FEEDING IS NOT AN EXTRAORDINARY MEASURE

Such a death would certainly be an example of technological hubris, but no one should believe that this is routine care for elderly patients with terminal conditions. The extreme, high-tech procedures imagined by ordinary people are rarely the subject of debate; it is simple feeding tubes and common antibiotics that are labeled "unnatural" by "ethicists"—in the thought that the life which they sustain is also unnatural and should not be continued. Feeding tubes are artificial and unnatural, of course, although they are low-tech and simple to use. They are necessary only for a person who cannot swallow. In most cases, spoon-feeding can be, and used to be, done instead, though it is more expensive. Spoon-feeding must be done by hand and spoon-fed diets have to taste good. It is unfair to blame feeding tubes for keeping people alive when many patients (including even some in PVS) could be nourished by other methods. This does not change the fact that feeding tubes are unnatural. But the nature of man is to live in an unnatural environment. There are many people in our society who are kept alive by unnatural technology. There are many people with mild chronic diseases or physical handicaps who are not robust enough to live without electricity, running water, air-conditioning, cars, microwaves, and telephones. Placed in the natural environment of a third world country, they would soon die—unless, of course, someone was willing to care for them. But is such care "natural"? Is it natural for a person or family or society to assume the burdensome care of an adult who will never get better? Is it more natural to help a crippled adult limp to the toilet than to diaper and wash an incontinent adult? Is spoon-feeding a paralyzed man who can only open his mouth and swallow more natural than tube-feeding a paralyzed man who can turn his head and smile?

Perhaps we should ask a different question. Perhaps we should ask, "Is it natural or unnatural for man to use technology to increase his physical comfort?"

Having spent a fair amount of time dehydrated and malnourished, I can confidently say that hydration is far more pleasant than the opposite. Anyone who doubts this can forgo fluids for a few days or nourishment for a few weeks and experience the reality. And after my experiences with staph infections, I would want antibiotics even if I were dying of cancer.

Reprinted by permission of Chuck Asay and Creators Syndicate.

Of course, there is an art to the practice of medicine, part of which involves looking at the patient as well as the chart, and knowing what will help and what will hurt the whole person. There may be times when antibiotics cannot be given, perhaps because the side effects are worse than the staph or because the kidneys or liver cannot take the strain. There may be times when a cancerous mass or fluid retention causes tube feeding to be painful. And there comes a time when the gut and kidneys shut down. The body cannot use food and water after that point, and death is very close. But I cannot understand taking away food and fluid before the body itself decides to quit.

Although food, water, and antibiotics add greatly to a patient's comfort, there are still people who fear a technological "bad death." They have, I think, two reasons for their fear. Hospital deaths with IVs and feeding tubes are the only deaths they see, and, with or without medical technology, dying tends to be a long and painful struggle. This is not the fault of the feeding tube. It is nature's fault. Our bodies are constructed to fight death. Everything from our bone marrow to the wax in our ears continually defends the body against invasion, attacking invaders who have breached the barriers and repairing injury. Death may be natural in that it is part of nature, but our bodies do not find it so. It is natural for them to struggle against death until there is nothing left to fight with, and anyone watching the struggle is going to be upset. It is hard to watch even when the patient is kept as comfortable as possible—even harder if the patient is in pain.

I believe this is the strongest reason for the fear of a technological bad death. Many of us who have lost friends or relatives have seen them suffer great pain. Unfortunately, we have sometimes seen doctors or nurses treating dying patients as though they were merely surgical cases, allowed only so much sedation every four hours. It may well seem more compassionate to starve and dehydrate a patient rather than to allow him to live on in such pain. And food and water are, of course, futile for a dying patient. But so is bedding, so is clothing, so is shelter. None of these will cure disease or prevent death except for the death that results when they are taken away. We can take away the bedding and the clothing and leave the helpless patient naked, so he dies of hypothermia or pneumonia. We can take away the artificial shelter of the hospital and leave the patient in a natural setting, so he dies of exposure. Or we can take away his food and water so he starves and dies of thirst. We can then soothe our consciences by saying that we have not killed anyone or intended anyone's death, but merely allowed nature to take its course.

REMOVING FEEDING TUBES CAN CAUSE A PAINFUL DEATH

But we are in control of nature. We decide what we will take away, and when, and from whom. Nature becomes our tool and does our dirty work for us, allowing us to feel blameless as we pull the stomach tube and disconnect the IV.

Most ordinary people, however, know there is a difference between omission and abandonment. They do not accept the idea, so popular with those who would remove food and fluid, that taking away a helpless person's food and water is morally superior to giving him a lethal injection. My distant cousin, a man with cancer, died from the removal of his food and water.

His sister was not allowed to be in on the decision, but she watched him die in torment. While he was still able to feel pain, he was racked by agonizing muscle spasms. When he was finally dead, he was so contorted that the undertaker was unable to make him presentable. His sister, a registered nurse, considered it the most horrible death she had ever seen.

Of course, those who would remove food and fluid do not wish to torture the helpless: therefore, I can only assume that they have no idea of the quiet torment of starvation and dehydration. Doctors may say that it doesn't hurt, but knowledge of suffering cannot be gained second-hand. I do not understand how a headache feels by reading about constricted blood vessels. I know how those blood vessels feel because I have a headache. My experiences with starvation and dehydration have not encouraged me to think of them as a comfortable alternative to the "bad death" of feeding tubes, nor as a superior rival to the swift, painless, merciful death promised by those who support euthanasia.

WITHDRAWING FOOD FROM THE PERMANENTLY COMATOSE

But those who would remove food and fluid do not stop with the terminal patient. They are also concerned with those leading a technological "bad life"—those in PVS. They feel that many people are afraid of ending up in such a state, and this fear encourages grassroots support of euthanasia.

I agree about the fear, but I believe it has a different cause. I have had high school students express concern about ending up in PVS, perhaps because they have been taught that it can result from drinking and driving. But the older people I know are simply afraid of helplessness. In the celebrated case of Christine Busalacchi, the St. Louis papers and TV stations were full of debate on whether her cerebral cortex was functioning. The case was an example of medical arrogance—CAT scans and neurological tests were used to measure a human relationship, and the testimony of caregivers from different institutions was ignored. But most of the people I talked to about the case did not care about her cerebral cortex. They did not care whether or not Christine was capable of experiencing pleasure or pain or responding to the love of others. They saw a helpless person dependent on others for her care, without control over her basic functions, and they did not like the picture.

Some of those concerned with this problem would not remove food and fluid from those who are not terminal and who have a functioning cerebral cortex. But the ordinary people I am referring to do not want to live with a damaged but functioning cerebral cortex that results in limited or deranged behavior. They dread living with severe Alzheimer's Disease—unable to recognize family and friends, unable to care for themselves, obsessed with the idea that someone is stealing their clothes. Many feel the same about strokes and fear mental impairment, loss of bodily control and simple dignity.

The publicity surrounding PVS cases has certainly been used by the media as a stimulus for the euthanasia movement, but there is also a great deal of quiet publicity—in newspapers, in women's magazines, and on local TV stations—that shows an ugly picture of the lives of those who simply need care. These stories deal with the problems of living with Alzheimer's Disease or stroke damage, the abuse of the elderly by their children, nursing home horror stories, the cost of long-term care, and the problems of those who must work, care for their children, and also care for elderly relatives. The message is often veiled but clear—there is a strong possibility that the last years of life will be spent in a miserable state, devoid of human dignity, plagued by demented behavior and physical suffering, costly and burdensome to others. How much kinder it seems to give such people the blessing of a swift, painless, dignified death.

This is the great attraction of euthanasia: to spare ourselves the experience of the body's struggle with death. I believe that the only way to resist the seduction of euthanasia is to care—to nurse the terminal person with love, to manage pain better, to recognize and respond to the dying person as Ruth or Helen or Fred instead of as a problem to be solved. Dying people do not lose their personalities or their humanity. They still like lemon sherbet, fingernail polish, baseball news. They still need humor, consideration, loving caresses, and companionship.

CARING FOR THE DISABLED IS IMPORTANT

Dying people can and should be nurtured—but what of the helpless person who is not dying? I believe the same things hold true. The quality of the helpless person's life depends to a great extent on the care received—on the competence, cheerfulness, and affection of those who do the caregiving. My grandfather, who lived for twelve years in a nursing home, was so paralyzed from the effects of Parkinson's Disease that he could hardly open his mouth, yet the nurses loved him and his family came and came often, bringing all the grandkids for him to enjoy— once even celebrating Christmas in his room so he could watch them open presents.

And as for people in PVS, we will never know what their damaged brains are capable of relearning unless we are willing to nurture them. It is highly unscientific, at the very least, to think that we know everything we need to know about the brain and that any behavior from a PVS patient that contradicts the current theory of "vegetablism" is irrelevant. Neurological tests and CAT scans do not constitute a theory. The behavior of the patient linked with the tests and scan are what we use to construct the theory. And since there is conflicting evidence about behavior, and since diagnosis is not infallible, it is inhumane to deprive people of food and water simply because current theory holds that they cannot feel it.

If our current theory is wrong, we will have caused a "bad death." Starvation and dehydration do cause suffering. They add to the cruelty and ugliness of death and reinforce the idea that the helpless person is no longer a member of the human family. I am sure that some will say that the sufferings of thirst and starvation can be alleviated, but it is asking a great deal of nurses and doctors to expect them to take away food and water and then treat the problems caused by taking away food and water. And if some compassionate doctors or nurses make an effort to discover effective sedation to remove the torments of thirst, if they try to keep the patient's electrolytes balanced and carefully adjust the amount of food and fluid (still using the feeding tube) in order to lessen the suffering as much as possible, then nature is no longer allowed to take its course. This death also becomes technological—and for the same reason: to make the patient as comfortable as possible while he dies.

THE SLIPPERY SLOPE TOWARD EUTHANASIA

If we are serious about fighting the euthanasia movement, I believe we must fight the idea that our status as members of the human family depends on our health, that under certain circumstances we will no longer be nurtured, our basic needs will purposely be ignored, and we will be abandoned to suffer and die. If we establish the idea that people no longer have lifetime membership in the human family, the practice of abandonment could become widespread—strongly encouraged perhaps by insurance carriers to cut costs. Then we may find ourselves no longer able to choose to die a death befitting the dignity of a man living to the end of his natural life, surrounded by concern for his comfort, and given the basic care his body still needs. Instead, our death will resemble the death of an unwanted dog who is abandoned by his owners and left to die of starvation and dehydration. Every responsible pet owner knows that it is a cruel fate for an animal, no matter how old or sick. And those who see a worn-out horse or an old dog left without food and water can call the police.

But if we decide that it is acceptable to treat humans worse than we treat animals, it should not surprise us if many people at the grassroots level decide that as long as they have to die like a dog, they would rather not suffer the fate of an abandoned stray. We should not be surprised if they work long and hard for the legal right to be quickly and painlessly "put to sleep" by the family "vet." Once this is accomplished, the evil inherent in such a practice will become all too apparent. As any member of the humane society can testify, disease and infirmity are not the only, or even the most common, reasons why Fido is put to sleep.

PERIODICAL BIBLIOGRAPHY

The following articles have been selected to supplement the diverse views presented in this chapter. Addresses are provided for periodicals not indexed in the *Readers' Guide to Periodical Literature*, the *Alternative Press Index*, the *Social Sciences Index*, or the *Index to Legal Periodicals and Books*.

Norwood R. Anderson	"The Enemy: A Biblical Case for Fighting Death Throughout Our Lives," *Christianity Today*, February 7, 1994.
Marcia Angell	"After Quinlan: The Dilemma of the Persistent Vegetative State," *New England Journal of Medicine*, May 26, 1994. Available from 10 Shattuck St., Boston, MA 02115-6094.
Daniel Callahan	"Cramming for Your Finals: Make Death a Part of Life," *Commonweal*, July 16, 1993.
Daniel Callahan	"Our Fear of Dying: How Our Determination to Control Mortality Has Distorted the Mission of Medicine," *Newsweek*, October 4, 1993.
Dudley Clendinen	"When Death Is a Blessing and Life Is Not," *New York Times*, February 5, 1996.
Geraldine Gorman	"My Father's Left Hand: A Death He Did Not Deserve," *Commonweal*, July 16, 1993.
Jack D. McCue	"The Naturalness of Dying," *JAMA*, April 5, 1995. Available from American Medical Association, 515 N. State St., Chicago, IL 60610.
LaVonne Neff	"To Dust You Will Return," *U.S. Catholic*, March 1996.
Bette-Jane Raphael	"Was I Right to Let My Mother Die?" *Glamour*, March 1995.
Robert J. Samuelson	"The Cost Of Compassion," *Washington Post National Weekly Edition*, July 24–30, 1995. Available from Reprints, 1150 15th St. NW, Washington, DC 20071.
Gail Shafarman	"The Second Door," *Family Therapy Networker*, January/February 1996. Available from 8528 Bradford Rd., Silver Spring, MD 20910.
Wesley J. Smith	"Eating His Words," *National Review*, December 11, 1995.
Wesley J. Smith	"Killing Grounds," *National Review*, March 6, 1995.

CHAPTER 2

DO INDIVIDUALS HAVE A RIGHT TO DIE?

CHAPTER PREFACE

While opinion polls show that a majority of Americans approve of physician-assisted suicide and want it to be legalized, most doctors say they would not assist a person to prematurely end his or her life. Influenced by the prevailing code of medical ethics, many physicians maintain that it is wrong to hasten the death of terminally ill patients. But a growing number argue that if it will prevent undue suffering, assisting patients who rationally choose to commit suicide is acceptable.

Among those seeking to legalize assisted suicide is Timothy E. Quill, a physician in Rochester, New York, whose 1993 book *Death and Dignity: Making Choices and Taking Charge* describes his decision to help a patient dying from leukemia end her life. Under current standards of medical ethics, Quill notes, terminally ill patients may refuse life-prolonging treatment and doctors may legally withdraw or withhold life support from dying patients. "Why, then," he asks, "if a suffering patient who is not on life support chooses to end his life, does society [condemn it as] 'suicide,' or even 'killing'?" Quill asserts that in order to alleviate painful and undignified suffering, doctors should be legally allowed to prescribe lethal doses of medication to dying patients who request them.

However, many doctors object to the legalization of physician-assisted suicide, arguing that it violates traditional medical ethics. Leon R. Kass, a physician and professor of medicine and bioethics at the University of Chicago, maintains that there is a clear distinction between removing life support to allow a terminally ill patient to die and assisting the suicide of a patient. When a doctor withholds or removes life support, Kass explains, the patient's death results from his or her fatal illness. But when a doctor prescribes a lethal dose of medication to a patient, he contends, the doctor's actions—rather than the results of terminal illness—are the cause of the patient's death. Though it is permissible to remove life-support equipment that may be a burden to a dying patient, Kass argues, it is unethical and should remain illegal for doctors to take actions that are intended to hasten the deaths of patients. Physicians "must care for the dying, not make them dead," he concludes.

Though physician-assisted suicide may eventually be legalized by popular vote or by the courts, physicians will still have to struggle with ethical concerns about the deaths of terminally ill patients. The viewpoints in the following chapter examine some of the ethical and legal questions regarding the individual's right to die.

| "Our Constitution ... protect[s]
people's right to die as well as to
live."

THE CONSTITUTION PROTECTS THE RIGHT TO DIE

Part I: Ronald Dworkin, Part II: Leonard John Deftos

In Part I of the following two-part viewpoint, Ronald Dworkin argues that the constitutional protection of privacy outlined in *Roe v.Wade*, the 1973 Supreme Court decision that legalized abortion, extends to decisions by competent patients to hasten their own deaths. He maintains that counter to the objections of pro-life protesters, constitutional protection of the right to die will not lead to involuntary euthanasia. In Part II, Leonard John Deftos contends that the right to physician assistance in hastening one's own death has been established by previous Supreme Court decisions regarding advance directives, which protect the right to refuse unwanted medical treatment. Dworkin is a law professor at New York University and the author of *Life's Dominion: An Argument About Abortion, Euthanasia, and Individual Freedom*. Deftos, who holds an M.D. and a J.D., is a professor of medicine at the University of California, San Diego and at the San Diego Veterans Administration Medical Center.

As you read, consider the following questions:

1. According to Dworkin, how does the "slippery slope" argument contradict common sense?
2. In Dworkin's words, what is the "deeper" conviction that underlies opposition to euthanasia and abortion?
3. How does Deftos define the doctrine of the "double effect"?

Part I: Ronald Dworkin, "When Is It Right to Die?" *New York Times*, May 17, 1994. Copyright ©1994 The New York Times Company. Reprinted by permission. Part II: Leonard John Deftos, "Is There a Constitutional Right to Die?" *San Diego Union-Tribune*, January 10, 1997. Reprinted by permission of the author.

I

A lawsuit [*Compassion in Dying v. State of Washington*] decided in Seattle in May 1994 may well become the *Roe v. Wade* of euthanasia. Striking down a 140-year-old Washington State law, Federal District Court Judge Barbara Rothstein declared that as long as they are competent, terminally ill patients have a constitutional right to enlist a willing doctor's help in killing themselves. She decided, that is, that laws against assisted suicide, which exist in almost every state, are unconstitutional. Once again, the courts are at the center of a bitter moral and religious controversy.

Americans have been arguing about euthanasia for decades. Voters in two states, Washington and California, have rejected measures legalizing euthanasia in fairly close votes; another such measure is expected to be on the ballot in Oregon later this year. [Oregon's Death with Dignity Act was approved by voters in November 1994, but a restraining order has kept it from becoming law.] In Michigan, a special statute was passed to stop Dr. Jack Kevorkian from helping patients to die, but a jury refused to convict him of violating that statute even though he virtually admitted he had.

If Judge Rothstein's decision, or a similar one, is upheld in the Supreme Court [which heard arguments in the case in January 1997 and is expected to issue a ruling in Summer 1997], the Constitution will preempt part of this sprawling debate: every state will have to recognize that though it can regulate doctor-assisted suicide, it can't prohibit it altogether. That result will outrage millions of conscientious citizens who think euthanasia an abomination in any form.

THE RIGHT TO PRIVACY IN ABORTION AND DEATH

Judge Rothstein said her decision on euthanasia was "almost" compelled by the Supreme Court's 1992 decision in *Planned Parenthood v. Casey*, which reaffirmed *Roe v. Wade*. In *Casey*, the Court declared: "Matters involving the most intimate and personal choices a person may make in a lifetime . . . are central to the liberty protected by the 14th Amendment. At the heart of liberty is the right to define one's own concept of existence, of meaning, of the universe, and of the mystery of human life." Judge Rothstein observed, correctly, that the freedom of a competent dying person to hasten his or her own death falls under that description at least as clearly as does the right of a pregnant woman to choose abortion.

Many opponents of euthanasia try to distinguish the two issues by appealing to a "slippery-slope" argument. They say, for example, that voluntary euthanasia will so habituate doctors to killing that they may begin executing sick, old, unwanted people whose care is expensive but who plainly want to live.

This contradicts common sense. Of course doctors know the moral difference between helping people who beg to die and killing those who want to live. If anything, ignoring the pain of terminal patients pleading for death rather than trying to help seems more likely to dull a doctor's humane instincts.

Some critics worry about the practice in the Netherlands, where doctors have given lethal injections to unconscious or incompetent terminal patients who did not explicitly ask to die. But Judge Rothstein's opinion applies only to assisted suicide, which demands an explicit request, and even if a legislature were to allow for such injection for patients incapable of taking pills or killing themselves in some other humane way, it could stipulate that an explicit request was still essential.

STATES HAVE THE POWER TO COUNTER A SLIPPERY SLOPE

A more plausible version of the slippery-slope argument worries that if euthanasia is legalized, dying people whose treatment is expensive or burdensome may ask for help in committing suicide only because they feel guilty, and that family members may perhaps try to coax or shame them toward that decision. But states plainly have the power to guard against requests influenced by guilt, depression, poor care or financial worries. (The main plaintiff in the Washington State case, the group Compassion in Dying, offers to assist only terminal patients who have repeated their request three times and have expressed no ambivalence or uncertainty.)

States also have the power to discourage distasteful, near assembly-line suicides like those arranged by Dr. Kevorkian. Patients go to him, and juries acquit him, only because there is no better alternative.

No set of regulations can be perfect. But it would be perverse to force competent people to die in great pain or in a drugged stupor for that reason, accepting a great and known evil to avoid the risk of a speculative one. In 1990 the Supreme Court held that states must respect some form of "living will" that allows people to specify in advance that certain procedures not be used to keep them alive, even though patients could be coaxed or shamed into signing such documents.

Some doctors already engage in a covert practice that is much more open to abuse than a scheme of voluntary euthanasia would be: they deliberately give dying patients fatal doses of painkilling drugs. But nobody thinks that this is a good reason to withhold all dangerous painkillers from terminal patients in torment.

THE CONSTITUTIONAL RIGHT TO DIE

Like the decision of whether or not to have an abortion, the decision how and when to die is one of "the most intimate and personal choices a person may make in a lifetime," a choice "central to personal dignity and autonomy" [Casey v. Planned Parenthood, 1992]. A competent terminally ill adult, having lived nearly the full measure of his life, has a strong liberty interest in choosing a dignified and humane death rather than being reduced at the end of his existence to a childlike state of helplessness, diapered, sedated, incontinent. How a person dies not only determines the nature of the final period of his existence, but in many cases, the enduring memories held by those who love him.

Stephen Reinhardt, Compassion in Dying v. State of Washington, March 6, 1996.

These slippery-slope arguments, then, are very weak ones. They seem only disguises for the deeper convictions that actually move most opponents of euthanasia. Matthew Habiger, president of Human Life International, a "pro-life" organization, denounced the Compassion in Dying decision in terms that made those deeper convictions explicit. "The march toward a complete anti-life philosophy," he said, "can now be easily mapped: from contraception to abortion to euthanasia. Once life is no longer treated as a sacred gift from God, a society inevitably embraces death in all its forms."

In this view, all euthanasia—even when fully voluntary and rational—is wrong because human life has an objective, intrinsic value as well as subjective value for the person whose life it is, and euthanasia dishonors that intrinsic value. It is precisely this conviction that underlies most opposition to abortion as well. Many people, particularly those who agree with Mr. Habiger that human life is a divine gift, believe that ending it deliberately (except, perhaps, as punishment) is always the most profound insult to life's objective value.

EUTHANASIA SUPPORTERS VALUE QUALITY OF LIFE

But it would be wrong to think that those who are more permissive about abortion and euthanasia are indifferent to the value of life. Rather, they disagree about what respecting that value means. They think that in some circumstances—when a fetus is terribly deformed, for example—abortion may show more respect for life than childbirth would. And they think that dying with dignity shows more respect for their own life—better fits their sense of what is really important in and about human existence—than ending their life in long agony or senseless sedation.

Our Constitution takes no sides in these ancient disputes about life's "meaning." But it does protect people's right to die as well as to live, so far as possible, in the light of their own intensely personal convictions about "the mystery of human life." It insists that these values are too central to personality, too much at the core of liberty, to allow a majority to decide what everyone must believe.

Of course the law must protect people who think it would be appalling to be killed, even if they had only painful minutes to live. But the law must also protect those with the opposite conviction: that it would be appalling not to be offered an easier, calmer death with the help of doctors they trust. Making a person die in a way that others approve, but that affronts his own dignity, is a serious, unjustified, unnecessary form or tyranny.

II

Bad cases lead to good law, and in medicine, tough cases lead to scrutinized decisions. Whether adages or canards, both of these statements apply to the two right-to-die cases [Quill v. Vacco and Compassion in Dying v. State of Washington] that were argued before the U.S. Supreme Court in January 1997.

The right requested by the cases—to choose and hasten the time of one's death—is not the "sea change" proclaimed by its opponents. The right is rather a continuation of the trajectory of the law and practice of medicine toward personal autonomy, a trajectory that began in midcentury and was propelled in 1976 by the national notoriety of the plight of Karen Ann Quinlan and again in 1990 by the similar plight of Nancy Cruzan.

The Cases of Quinlan and Cruzan

Quinlan, a young woman in a persistent vegetative state, was granted a constitutional right to refuse treatment by the New Jersey Supreme Court after a long and agonizing delay.

Prior to this case, such medical decisions were often made with a paternalistic and unctuous attitude by courts and physicians. Fearing prosecution and moral reprimand, physicians had medically intervened with life-sustaining procedures against the will of their patients until the courts mercifully, but belatedly, interceded.

In the case of Cruzan, the U.S. Supreme Court identified a constitutionally protected liberty interest in rejecting treatment that already had been initiated. In the Cruzan decision, the right to refuse treatment was extended to the right to reject treatment, and the two became legally indistinguishable liberties.

Thus, from a constitutional perspective, there are no substantial differences along the continuum of withholding life-sustaining medical treatment, withdrawing such treatment, and, as the cases before the Court show, physician-assisted suicide. All serve the same intent—to hasten death.

Physician-assisted suicide does not approximate forbidden euthanasia any more than the current medical practice that some physicians use in the treatment of their terminally ill patients, practices that are ethically and medically sanctioned.

FROM LIVING WILLS TO ASSISTED SUICIDE

The common-law liberties identified by Quinlan and Cruzan became formalized by legislatively created "living wills," "advance directives" and "durable powers of attorney," whereby patients could identify in advance their wishes about life-sustaining treatments.

Among the choices available to patients under these legal documents is the "do-not-resuscitate" order to physicians. This request is tantamount to a choice to hasten one's death and may be regarded as a close approximation to a request for assisted suicide. If a physician ignores such a request, he or she can, in many jurisdictions, be subject to a "wrongful life" lawsuit.

This trajectory of personal autonomy regarding medical intervention is hypocritically intersected by the "double-effect" doctrine. This doctrine, sanctioned by most professional medical organizations, including the American Medical Association, allows physicians to treat the pain of a terminally ill patient with a dose of drugs that can cause death, as long as their ostensible intent is to treat pain.

This legally and medically accepted doctrine of "terminal sedation," which has so far protected Dr. Jack Kevorkian at his trials, in fact comes closer to euthanasia than does assisted suicide, since the physician, not the patient, administers the drug of death.

Thus, the two cases before the U.S. Supreme Court are not such profound changes in medical-legal policy. They are rather on the common-law continuum of Quinlan and Cruzan and the statutory continuum of living wills and advance directives.

They also present a more honest and open option to the competent, terminally ill patient than always gruesome and often prolonged "terminal sedation." Even though these two cases grew from different legal limbs of the 14th Amendment—equal protection and liberty rights—the basic issue they bring before the Supreme Court is whether or not a right to physician assistance for the terminally ill patient who competently chooses to hasten the time of his or her death should be *absolutely* prohibited.

THE RIGHTS OF STATES TO REGULATE ASSISTED SUICIDE

As argued by Harold Glucksberg and Timothy Quill [the doctors in the assisted suicide cases before the Supreme Court], a balancing analysis is the correct way to assess any state interests that compete with the individual's liberty interest. An individual's liberty interest in hastening his or her death is at its nadir when that person is young and healthy and at its peak when he or she is terminally ill.

Conversely, the burden of the state on that liberty is greatest when the liberty is prohibited, lesser when it is regulated, and lesser still when it is absent. The ultimate constitutional question is whether sufficient justification exists for intrusion by the government into the "realm of a person's liberty, dignity and freedom."

If the balance favors the state, then the given statute—whether it regulates the exercise of a due-process liberty interest or prohibits that exercise to some degree—is constitutional. If the balance favors the individual, then the statute, whatever its justifications, violates the individual's due-process liberty rights and must be declared unconstitutional.

Opponents of the right to physician-assisted suicide would rather the Supreme Court stay silent on the issue before it and leave any right of the terminally ill to control the circumstances of their death to the 50 state legislatures.

The predictable failure of such an approach is illustrated by the attempts of California, Washington and Oregon to so address the issue and the conflicting legal results of these attempts. Oregon voters passed in 1994 a referendum to allow physician-assisted suicide, while the voters of Washington in 1991 and California in 1992 narrowly defeated such measures, and several other states have considered similar measures.

Oregon courts deemed their law permitting physician-assisted suicide unconstitutional, while, in contrast, judges in the New York [Quill] and Washington cases declared unconstitutional those states' laws that prohibit physician-assisted suicide.

THE SUPREME COURT SHOULD DECIDE

It is just such a legal morass that warrants a unifying Supreme Court decision. Contrary to the view of opponents of this right, this is exactly the function of the federal judiciary, and it has been so at least since Article III was included in the Constitution in 1787, and certainly since Chief Justice John Marshall's 1803 decision in *Marbury v. Madison.*

The progress and progression of our legal and medical ethos should culminate in the constitutional circumscription and protection, not prohibition, of such a right. And "slippery slope" arguments aside, such a right need neither become a license for euthanasia nor a widely applied law since it will pertain only to the small minority of terminally ill patients who voluntarily choose physician-assisted suicide.

Although it is abhorrent for a physician to contemplate participation in the death of her patient, a carefully crafted, limited and regulated right to physician assistance for the terminally-ill in choosing the circumstances of their death could bring compassion, order and dignity to this most difficult time. At your deathbed, would you rather be with Dr. Kevorkian in the back of a van or with a hopefully caring but legally accountable physician like the kindly Dr. Quill?

"The judicial discovery of a sweeping
constitutional right to die is
analytically unconvincing and
politically indefensible."

THE CONSTITUTION DOES NOT PROTECT THE RIGHT TO DIE

Jeffrey Rosen

Proponents of physician-assisted suicide argue that the right to privacy established in Supreme Court decisions regarding abortion and medical treatment extends to the right to die. In the following viewpoint, Jeffrey Rosen contends that past Supreme Court decisions regarding the right to refuse medical treatment established a legal distinction between killing a patient and allowing him or her to die. By making this distinction, he maintains, these rulings prohibit physician participation in euthanasia. Further, Rosen argues, the legalization of abortion was based on a woman's right to privacy in decisions about reproduction, which cannot logically be extended to decisions about death and dying. Rosen is the legal affairs editor of the New Republic.

As you read, consider the following questions:

1. In Rosen's opinion, why is Judge Reinhardt incorrect in suggesting that the Supreme Court has recognized a liberty interest in hastening one's own death?
2. According to the Planned Parenthood v. Casey decision, quoted by the author, what personal decisions are protected by the Constitution?

From "What Right to Die?" by Jeffrey Rosen, New Republic, June 24, 1996. Reprinted by permission of the New Republic; ©1996, The New Republic, Inc.

It's hard not to be moved by emotional accounts of how laws prohibiting assisted suicide can drive pain-wracked people to desperate ends. In May 1995, in *The New Yorker*, Andrew Solomon wrote eloquently about how he and his brother helped their mother take sleeping pills to spare her the final agonies of ovarian cancer, an ordeal made even more harrowing by the fear of prosecution. All of the jurors who acquitted Dr. Jack Kevorkian in May 1996 similarly said they were influenced by videotapes in which two women suffering from chronic pain described their anguish and pleaded to be allowed to die. (The jurors were unmoved by the fact that the ailments were not fatal.) Confronted with heartbreaking stories like these, it's tempting to conclude that all laws barring competent citizens from dying with dignity should be repealed or invalidated. And, indeed, when two federal appeals courts, during 1996, struck down state laws in New York and Washington prohibiting physician-assisted suicide, the judges were widely praised for their statesmanship and humanity.

THE DIFFERENCE BETWEEN ABORTION AND EUTHANASIA

But, in fact, the judicial discovery of a sweeping constitutional right to die is analytically unconvincing and politically indefensible. The decisions rely heavily on the similarities between abortion and euthanasia, both of which, to use Ronald Dworkin's typically abstract formulation, involve "choices for death." Both euthanasia and abortion inspire profound religious and moral disputes; both have been, at certain times in American history, prohibited by the states; and the case for each becomes more or less compelling at different points in the life cycle. But creating constitutional rights by analogy is often treacherous, as the Supreme Court discovered in the wake of *Roe v. Wade*, when it was witheringly criticized for expanding its earlier cases concerning the privacy of the marital bedroom into an apparently unrelated right of doctors to perform first-trimester abortions in hospitals. By blithely repeating the errors of *Roe*, and expanding the narrow right to refuse unwanted medical treatment into a much broader right to hasten one's own death, the assisted suicide decisions show the dangers of constitutional abstraction. What follows is a narrative of how a constitutional right is invented.

Until the judicial decisions in 1996, America's euthanasia debate was organized around a series of carefully maintained distinctions. The most basic right, now recognized by the Supreme Court, Congress and the state legislatures, is the right to refuse unwanted medical treatment, such as feeding tubes and hydration. Less widely accepted is assisted suicide, still criminal in thirty-four states, which occurs when a doctor prescribes medication that may ease pain or cause death (the double effect), and the patient administers the lethal dose himself. Most controversial is "voluntary passive euthanasia," which takes place when the doctor, rather than the incapacitated patient, administers the lethal dose with the patient's consent.

In March 1996, in San Francisco, the U.S. Court of Appeals for the Ninth Circuit impatiently swept aside these painstaking distinctions and became the first federal appeals court in the country to recognize a constitutional right to "determine the time and manner of one's own death." Writing for eight members of the Court, Judge Stephen Reinhardt struck down a Washington state law prohibiting physician-assisted suicide, and draped himself in Justice Harry Blackmun's mantle. "In deciding right-to-die cases, we are guided by the Court's approach to the abortion cases," he declared, and proceeded to discover a constitutional right to die in the interstices of the Constitution's due process clause. . . .

REFUSING MEDICAL TREATMENT VS. ASSISTED SUICIDE

First, he invokes the Supreme Court's 1990 *Cruzan* opinion, in which the parents of Nancy Cruzan, a patient in a persistent vegetative state, sought to remove her feeding tube, even though the patient herself had not left a living will. Chief Justice William Rehnquist assumed, for the sake of argument, that competent people have a "constitutionally-protected liberty interest in refusing unwanted medical treatment." But Rehnquist held that a state could require convincing evidence of a patient's wishes before requiring hospitals to pull the plug.

By recognizing a right to refuse medical treatment, Judge Reinhardt suggests expansively, the Supreme Court "necessarily recognize[d] a liberty interest in hastening one's own death." But in fact the Supreme Court did no such thing. The Court emphasized that each state has an "unqualified interest in the preservation of human life," and to illustrate this point, it noted that "the majority of states in this country have laws imposing criminal penalties on one who assists another to commit suicide." Far from questioning these laws, the Supreme Court explicitly appeared to endorse them.

The Supreme Court's distinction between refusing treatment and committing assisted suicide, between killing and letting die, is analytically coherent and nationally accepted. (In 1990, Congress codified the right to refuse medical treatment in the Federal Patient Self-Determination Act.) A long line of cases say that patients have a right to be protected against unwanted physical contact from doctors, which can be seen as a kind of violent battery or a violation of the principle of informed consent. Hooking people up to tubes against their will might also be seen as an unreasonable search or seizure of the body, prohibited by the Fourth Amendment. By contrast, a patient who wants to commit assisted suicide is not seeking to have a feeding tube withdrawn, but to have lethal medication applied. Prohibiting doctors from actively killing can hardly be considered as a bodily seizure or a battery.

Roe v. Wade Does Not Support the Right to Die

Perhaps recognizing the inadequacy of the *Cruzan* case as a fountainhead for his broad right to die, Reinhardt turns to the abortion cases. But, even on its own terms, Reinhardt's analogy between abortion and assisted suicide is implausible. The cases from which *Roe v. Wade* derived a constitutional right to abortion involved reproductive autonomy or marital privacy. All have been reconceived, in the years since *Roe*, as cases involving gender discrimination and the special burdens suffered by women during unwanted pregnancy. But the right to die has no logical connection to sexual autonomy or gender equality.

The only way Reinhardt can sustain his analogy between abortion and euthanasia is by characterizing the sexual privacy cases at the highest possible level of generalization: "A common thread running through these [abortion and contraception] cases is that they involve decisions that are highly personal and intimate, as well as of great importance to the individual. Certainly, few decisions are more personal, intimate, or important than the decision to end one's life, especially when the reason for doing so is to avoid excessive and protracted pain." But this analogy is too slippery to be convincing. For some citizens, no decision is more "personal, intimate, or important" than the decision to engage in homosexual conduct; but this choice, according to the Supreme Court, is not one the Constitution protects. And it's hard to imagine a democracy that would authorize judges to invent fundamental rights guided by nothing more than their own estimation of which decisions are "personal, intimate, or important."

Reinhardt quotes a passage from *Planned Parenthood v. Casey,* the 1992 abortion case: "At the heart of liberty is the right to define one's own concept of existence, of meaning, of the universe, and of the mystery of human life." This doesn't help matters.

Taken out of context, as Judge Robert Beezer emphasized dryly in dissent, the right to define one's own concept of existence "is so broad and melodramatic as to seem almost comical in its rhetorical flourish." But Reinhardt skirted over the preceding sentences in *Casey*, which emphasize that "our law affords constitutional protection to personal decisions relating to marriage, procreation, contraception, family relationships, child rearing, and education." Decisions about death are a different matter.

THERE IS NO CONSTITUTIONAL RIGHT TO DIE

Neither the 1976 *Quinlan* case nor the 1990 *Cruzan* case (the only one involving death, dying, and the "right to privacy" ever decided by the U.S. Supreme Court) nor any other case establishes an absolute or general right to die—a right to end one's life in any manner one sees fit. The only right or liberty that the so-called "right to die" cases have established is the right under certain circumstances to be disconnected from artificial life-support systems or, as many have called it, the right to die *a natural death*. Indeed, the *Quinlan* case explicitly distinguished between letting die, on the one hand, and both direct killing and assisted suicide on the other.

Yale Kamisar, *First Things*, December 1993.

The unbounded quality of Reinhardt's "right to hasten one's own death" is the best reason to reject it. In a series of prescient articles written since 1958, Yale Kamisar of the University of Michigan has argued convincingly that courts should decline to expand the narrow right to refuse unwanted medical treatment into a broader right to control the timing of one's own death, because the broader right has no logical stopping point. And Reinhardt's opinion vindicates Kamisar's most dramatic fears. Isn't a healthy but depressed person's decision to commit suicide just as "personal, intimate, or important" as a decision to commit suicide near the end of an incurable illness? Wouldn't the right to define "one's own concept of existence" protect the right of all citizens to kill themselves, for whatever reasons they please? Reinhardt anxiously denies that he means to endorse a right of active voluntary euthanasia, but his "liberty interest" has no principled limits.

EQUAL RIGHTS TO DIE

A month after Judge Reinhardt struck down Washington state's law prohibiting assisted suicide, three judges on the U.S. Court of Appeals for the Second Circuit struck down New York state's assisted suicide law. The New York judges went out of their way to repudiate the reasoning of Judge Reinhardt's opinion, which they found open-ended and unconvincing. But they reached the same result for different reasons. The majority opinion, written by Judge Roger Miner, held that New York denies its citizens the equal protection of the laws, because it fails to "treat equally all competent persons who are in the final stages of fatal illness and wish to hasten their deaths." By allowing terminally ill patients on life support to refuse unwanted medical treatment, but prohibiting terminally ill patients who are *not* on life support to "hasten their deaths" with the aid of their physicians, New York, according to Judge Miner, fails to treat "similarly circumstanced persons alike."

Judge Miner's theory raises the specter of the slippery slope even more alarmingly than Judge Reinhardt's theory. As Yale Kamisar pointed out in testimony before the House Judiciary Committee at the end of April 1996, if people off life support have to be treated as if they are "similarly circumstanced," to use Miner's jargon, to people *on* life support, why aren't patients who want to kill themselves with prescription drugs "similarly circumstanced" to patients who want to be strangled by their doctors? And how can this right be confined to the terminally ill? If New York has a duty to "treat equally all competent people who are in the final stages of fatal illness and wish to hasten their deaths," to use Miner's words again, isn't Kamisar correct that it would be similarly arbitrary to exclude people who suffer from Alzheimer's, severe depression or even arthritis?

There are good reasons, of course, why it was perfectly rational for the New York legislature to maintain the legal distinction between passively allowing a patient to die (which is permitted) and actively assisting in a patient's death (which is prohibited). As George Fletcher has argued, the distinction between action and omission is supported by the general reluctance, in American law, to hold people liable for their failure to prevent harm. And there's a broad medical, legal and philosophical consensus that stopping treatment should be considered not an action to kill but an omission to cure. Viewed in this light, assisted suicide violates the doctor's duty to avoid killing, while letting a patient die does not. . . .

POPULAR SUPPORT FOR THE RIGHT TO DIE?

The most jarring feature of these right-to-die opinions is their unabashed reliance on opinion polls. In a section of his opinion called "Current Societal Attitudes," Judge Reinhardt cites a 1994

Harris Poll indicating that 73 percent of the respondents favored legalizing physician-assisted suicide under certain conditions. "Polls have repeatedly shown that a large majority of Americans—sometimes nearing 90 percent—fully endorse recent legal changes granting terminally ill patients, and sometimes their families, the prerogative to accelerate their death by refusing or terminating treatment," Reinhardt enthuses. Judges are usually more subtle in their efforts to follow the election returns; but in any event, "current societal attitudes" are considerably more complicated than the various judges suggest. Three states have held referenda on proposals to allow physician-assisted suicide for the terminally ill. Voters in two states—Washington and California—rejected the proposal by margins of about 54 percent to 46 percent. Oregon voters are the only ones to endorse a decriminalization measure, by a narrow margin of 51 percent to 49 percent. Six state legislatures have recently rejected bills that would permit physician-assisted suicide, and no legislature has passed a decriminalization bill.

This popular ambivalence suggests that the abortion analogy, so heavily relied on by right-to-die advocates, is particularly inappropriate. David Garrow argues that in the abortion battles of the 1960s, professional opinion was substantially ahead of popular opinion: the American Medical Association supported liberalization of abortion laws, for example, while popular support for liberalization lagged behind. By contrast, Garrow notes, in the right-to-die battles today, popular opinion seems to be ahead of professional opinion: the American Medical Association opposes liberalization of assisted suicide laws, while Oregon voters and the Kevorkian jurors seem to support it. Of course, judges have no business reading the polls under any circumstances; but the deep national division on the assisted suicide question should make courts all the more hesitant to jump into the fray.

Assisted Suicide Laws Should Be Decided by States

All this is to say that the assisted suicide question, even more obviously than the abortion question, should be decided by the state legislatures and voters rather than by the courts. If left to their own devices, what are the states likely to decide? The policy question seems much harder than the constitutional question. Clearly, the laws prohibiting assisted suicide are rarely enforced: between 1950 and 1993, only eleven doctors in the United States were prosecuted for killing their terminally ill patients, and none went to prison. As one might expect, the infrequency with which the laws are enforced has dramatically reduced their deterrent effect: one in five doctors, according to a survey by the American Society of Internal Medicine, say they have helped their patients to commit suicide, as have one in five nurses, according to a more recent survey by *The New England Journal of Medicine*. This tacit public policy of refusing to prosecute physician-assisted suicides, except in the most suspicious cases, makes Judge Reinhardt's laments about the "onerous burden" of assisted suicide laws all the more hyperbolic.

In fact, the tension between what the law formally forbids and what society widely tolerates seems to have few social costs: with the exception of showmen like Dr. Kevorkian who openly court prosecution, doctors are relatively free to exercise their professional judgment in close cases. Why is there a burning need to repeal laws prohibiting assisted suicide? In *Aging and Old Age*, Judge Richard Posner argues that "permitting physician-assisted suicide . . . [in] cases of physical incapacity might actually reduce the number of suicides and postpone the suicides that occur." If the only choice is between killing themselves now and suffering later, patients who fear they might someday become so incapacitated that they would be unable to commit suicide on their own will kill themselves now. But, Posner argues, if the choice is between suicide now or physician-assisted suicide later, the aging may well choose suicide later, because there is a chance they will be proved to have been mistaken about their future suffering or incapacity.

THE DIFFICULTY OF REGULATING ASSISTED DEATH

If Judge Posner's utility curves are correct, legalizing assisted suicide might save a few lives and alleviate some pain. But the difficulty of reaching a consensus about appropriate regulations for physician-assisted suicide, especially given the hysteria of popular elections, suggests that it may be more sensible to leave matters as they are. The circuit courts in California and New York both agreed that the right to physician-assisted suicide can't be exercised without accompanying safeguards; and both circuits, in effect, ordered their state legislatures to adopt procedural regulations to protect against "errors and abuse." (What an odd constitutional right that judges invent, and then command the state legislatures to restrict!) But the gothic complexity of the model regulations cited by the courts should give a pragmatist pause. Judge Reinhardt, for example, commended the following safeguards to the Washington legislature: "witnesses to ensure voluntariness; reasonable, though short, waiting periods to prevent rash decisions; second medical opinions to confirm a patient's terminal status . . . psychological examinations to ensure that the patient is not suffering from momentary or treatable depression; reporting procedures that will aid in the avoidance of abuse." These suggestions may or may not be welcomed by the medical community; but surely doctors themselves are better qualified than state legislatures or judges to draft detailed codes of professional regulation.

It's naïve, perhaps, to be surprised at the brazen overconfidence of the New York and California judges, as they substituted their benign moral impulses for the more rigorous judgments of physicians, philosophers and the people's representatives. Maybe, given a chance to play king for a day, most of us would have trouble restraining ourselves, too. But I doubt that advocates of the right to die will thank the judges for this extravagant favor. By rushing to preempt a national debate that has only just begun, and in the most heavy-handed way possible, the California and New York decisions will surely energize the most extreme opponents of assisted suicide and fan the flames of their evangelical crusade. We've been down this road before, of course, but the aftermath of the abortion cases was supposed to have weaned us of the urge to venture down it again.

> "Many ... people will want the comfort of knowing that, if they so choose, a physician will be ready, willing, and able to help them ... by offering a death with dignity."

PHYSICIAN-ASSISTED DEATH SHOULD BE LEGALIZED

William H.A. Carr

William H.A. Carr is the former president of the Indiana chapter of the Hemlock Society, which advocates the right of terminally ill patients to choose to commit suicide. In the following viewpoint, Carr contends that there is growing support among doctors, churches, and the public for physician-assisted suicide. Many doctors already secretly and illegally help terminally ill patients end their suffering, he maintains. Physician-assisted death should be legalized, he argues, to ensure that patients who choose to can die with dignity.

As you read, consider the following questions:

1. According to the *Economist* magazine, cited by Carr, what is the slippery-slope argument advanced by opponents of assisted suicide?
2. According to the *New England Journal of Medicine*, quoted by the author, what percentage of doctors would be willing to assist a patient's suicide?

From "A Right to Die" by William H.A. Carr, *Saturday Evening Post*, September/October 1995. Reprinted by permission of the author.

There have been many absurd laws on the statute books, but some of the silliest have dealt with suicide. For many decades, attempted suicide was a crime, for which the punishment could be quite severe. In some jurisdictions, the punishment was death—thus, the government could achieve for the would-be suicide what he had been unable to accomplish for himself.

In most jurisdictions today, it is no longer a crime to attempt suicide—but it is a felony to help someone else do it. In other words, most jurisdictions now say that it is illegal to help someone else commit an act that is wholly legal. That doesn't make much sense, but then, neither do a lot of other laws.

TECHNOLOGY HAS PROLONGED DYING

However, these days, the issue of suicide has come to the fore, mostly because of the tremendous advances in medical technology over the past three decades. When today's middle-aged men and women were young, people generally died "when their time had come," as the saying had it. That's no longer true. Now people can be kept alive, in many instances long after they are "brain-dead," to use an expression that had to be invented because of the new medical technology. Worse still, they can be kept alive while fully conscious, although they may be in agony with no hope of recovery.

Because of the growing awareness of this possibility, a movement has sprung up, spearheaded by the Hemlock Society of the United States, to legalize physician-assisted death in such terminal cases. As usual, the media was slow to note the significance of this movement. Derek Humphry's book, Final Exit, has been described by some as a sort of "how-to-do-it" book on self-deliverance. When the book hit the No. 1 spot on the bestseller lists—where it remained for half a year—the media awoke to a startling new phenomenon. Suddenly, "death with dignity" was a cover story for Newsweek, a major event for coverage by the biggest newspapers, and the subject of earnest discussion by columnists.

Some tried to portray the issue in liberal-versus-conservative terms. Although it is true that such liberal columnists as Anna Quindlen and Ann Landers did come out in support of the Hemlock position, some people of impeccable conservative credentials did so as well.

CONSERVATIVE ARGUMENTS IN FAVOR OF ASSISTED SUICIDE

One was Ernest van den Haag, Ph.D., one of the academics who helped William F. Buckley and his National Review begin the conservative intellectual renaissance three decades ago. Van den

Haag, a philosopher and social scientist, is a distinguished scholar at the Heritage Foundation in Washington, D.C. In other words, the man is not exactly a "flaming liberal."

In a long Op-Ed piece in the *Wall Street Journal* (which some might consider a fairly conservative publication), van den Haag wrote: "More and more people reach advanced age. But for many, disability makes life a burden. Yet even when life is no longer desired, or consciously experienced, medicine can now prolong it. Although still fallible, diagnoses have become far more reliable than in the past; prognosis is fairly certain. Miracles—medical or religious—are rare. It is reasonable, then, to allow physicians to actively help end life when the patient so desires. . . . We should no longer ask whether assisted suicide, or mercy killing, should be allowed, but rather under what conditions."

Another conservative voice was that of the *Economist*, a highly respected British publication. It devoted several pages to the issue of physician-assisted death and tackled head-on the argument, by some opponents, that allowing doctors to do this would start society down a slippery slope that would end with involuntary euthanasia of the handicapped and anyone else who might be deemed a burden on society.

Said the *Economist*: "The slippery-slope argument deserves to be taken seriously. But some of those who advance it teeter precariously on a much more slippery slope of their own. The rights of the individual, they say, must be balanced against the interests of society: the taking of a life, at the patient's request, may seem acceptable in particular circumstances, but must be forbidden because it attacks values that bind society together. This way of thinking seems likable on the surface, but it sets the rights of the individual at naught: in that respect, it is philosophically related to the view that society should exterminate those who are a burden upon it. People who put society above the individual are indeed well-advised to be wary of assisted suicide."

RELIGIOUS SUPPORT FOR PHYSICIAN-AIDED DEATH

But what about the religious prohibition?

Several years ago, the Rev. Henry Van Dusen and his wife, Elizabeth, both of them in pain and with no prospect of recovery, joined in a suicide pact. The deaths were front-page news in the *New York Times* and most other newspapers because Van Dusen was president of Union Theological Seminary and one of the most respected theologians in the world. In a suicide note, Elizabeth Van Dusen wrote, "There are too many helpless old people who, without modern medicine, would have died, and we feel God would have allowed them to die when their time had come."

There are said to be six suicides mentioned in the Bible. The events that led to the suicides (for example, the betrayal of Jesus by Judas) are condemned, but the Bible's comments on each of the acts of suicide are neutral.

Although the hierarchy of the Roman Catholic Church has been emphatic in its opposition to euthanasia, spending millions to defeat such propositions at the polls, there are respected voices raised within that church in support of physician-assisted death. Dick Westley, philosopher and ethicist at Loyola University of Chicago, has published a book in which he says there is historical justification for church support of euthanasia, going back to the Middle Ages. "Euthanasia," he wrote, "is now seen as a tragic necessity required to protect human dignity."

PHYSICIANS SHOULD BE ALLOWED TO HELP SUFFERING PATIENTS

To think that all patients can be helped with more pain-relieving medication and treatment for depression is naïve. Some are forced to act on their own to end their lives rather than continue suffering. Prohibition of physician-assisted suicide handcuffs doctors who want to show compassion to patients whose bodies are irreversibly falling apart despite excellent medical care.

Timothy E. Quill, New York Times, July 23, 1994.

The Unitarian-Universalist Church has supported the concept of euthanasia for some time. The United Church of Christ has recently come around to a favorable view of the issue. Many other denominations are reexamining their beliefs.

There is reason to believe that many religious groups will end up endorsing death with dignity, because religions have a habit of changing. George Fox would be hard-put to recognize in today's Quakers the Religious Society of Friends that he founded. John Calvin would probably be bewildered by the Presbyterian Church of today. Even the Roman Catholic Church would be astonishing to a medieval pope.

This is not a criticism of these religious groups, but a tribute. The church was made for the living, not for the dead past; as times and social conditions change, revelation brings about appropriate changes. That's why the church endures.

PHYSICIANS' ATTITUDES TOWARD EUTHANASIA

If physician-assisted death were permitted, would doctors participate? Of course, some would not; everyone looks at this issue in the light of his or her own conscience. However, there are indications that some doctors would help certain patients die with dignity. The *New England Journal of Medicine* reported on a survey of medical doctors in the state of Washington that showed 54 percent thought euthanasia should be legal in some circumstances, and 40 percent said they would be willing to assist patients in that manner.

As every physician, in moments of candor, is willing to concede, euthanasia is being practiced by doctors all the time, right now, despite the risk of being charged with a felony and perhaps losing one's license to practice.

"Physician-assisted death is a common but private occurrence," *American Demographics* reported in 1991. It quoted Dr. David Rogers of the New York Hospital–Cornell Medical Center as saying, "I have let lots of people die. I've helped some of them die, although I'd deny that in court. And that's true of most of my colleagues."

Some doctors talk, in private, about how, when a terminally ill patient has pleaded for something to end the agony, they will put a bottle of pills by the bedside and warn the patient, "Now don't get confused during the night and take too many pills, because there are 50 in this bottle and 30 is the lethal dose." Other physicians resort to the "morphine drip," with the dosage gradually increasing until it becomes a fatal overdose.

These are doctors who want desperately to serve the best interests of their patients. They deserve to be honored. Nevertheless, there are dangers in the kind of situation we have today, in which good doctors must break the law to help their patients, with no safeguards or guidelines. That is why the laws need to be changed.

PUBLIC ATTITUDES TOWARD ASSISTED SUICIDE

That change is already underway. The first time the question of euthanasia was put to voters, in the state of Washington in 1992, 40 percent were in favor of physician-assisted death; 60 percent were opposed. That might sound like a loud and emphatic "no," but for a dramatically new idea that forces people to rethink some basic ideas about life and death, it was actually a surprisingly strong, though minority, response.

The following year, essentially the same proposition was put to the voters of California. Again it was defeated, but the percentages narrowed; 48 percent were in favor, 52 percent opposed.

Then, in November 1994, the voters of Oregon got a chance to express their views. This time, physician-assisted death won,

52 percent to 48 percent.

Under the Oregon law approved by the voters, the patient must be told that he or she has six months or less to live. The patient then must ask for medication to end his or her life; that request begins a 15-day waiting period. The attending physician must review the case, determine that the patient is mentally competent to make such a decision and is acting voluntarily, and inform the patient of other options besides euthanasia (hospice care, for example). Next of kin must be notified. The patient must be informed of the right to change his or her mind at any time. A second physician must be brought in to review the case and the entire process. If the patient is suffering from mental or emotional illness, or if depression is causing impaired judgment, he or she must be referred for counseling.

If all of these steps have been completed satisfactorily, the patient must voluntarily sign a written request, witnessed by two people, one of whom is not a relative or heir. Again, the patient must orally request lethal medication, and again the patient must be informed that the decision can be changed at any time. No less than 48 hours later, the patient can be given the lethal medication.

THE ISSUE IN THE COURTS

The new Oregon law is now being challenged in the federal courts [a court injunction prevents its enforcement until the issue is settled in the courts] with another case, from the state of Washington [Compassion in Dying v. State of Washington], in which physicians assert that the ban on assisting patients to die violates their right to practice medicine in the best interests of their patients (some of whom joined the lawsuit on the doctors' side). It is certain that the issue ultimately will end up before the U.S. Supreme Court, as any question of such importance should. [Compassion in Dying v. State of Washington and another assisted-suicide lawsuit, Quill v. Vacco, were argued before the Supreme Court in January 1997. A decision is expected in summer 1997.]

Regardless of the courtroom battles, there is little question that the tide of public opinion is running strongly in favor of euthanasia. A Gallup poll, reported in American Demographics magazine, indicated that 65 percent of the American public favored allowing doctors to help the terminally ill end their suffering if the patient and his or her family request it.

The changing demographics of our country contribute to this rising tide of public opinion. In 1950, there were 585,000 Americans 85 years of age and older. By 1990, that number had grown to 3.1 million. By the year 2005 the number will have reached 5.3 million. Many of those people will want the comfort of knowing that, if *they so choose*, a physician will be ready, willing, and able to help them escape agonizing pain and the humiliation of helplessness by offering a death with dignity.

"*As physicians, we should commit
ourselves to caring for human life,
not to deciding when it no longer
merits care.*"

PHYSICIAN-ASSISTED DEATH
SHOULD NOT BE LEGALIZED

Louis Vernacchio

Louis Vernacchio argues in the following viewpoint that physician
participation in assisted suicide violates the moral tenets of the
doctor's profession by blurring the distinction between allowing
terminally ill patients to die and killing them. Physician-assisted
suicide, he maintains, puts doctors in the untenable position of
deciding who should live and who should die. Doctors should
not engage in the practice even if it becomes legal, he concludes.
Vernacchio is a physician at Children's Hospital in Boston.

As you read, consider the following questions:

1. In Vernacchio's opinion, how does physician-assisted suicide
   contradict the doctor's duty to do no harm?
2. What are the four conditions that must be met under the
   principle of the double effect, according to the author?
3. In the author's view, what may happen if physician-assisted
   suicide attempts fail?

From "Physician-Assisted Suicide: Reflections of a Young Doctor" by Louis Vernacchio,
America, August 31, 1996. Reprinted by permission of the author.

I never imagined, when I entered medical school less than seven years ago, that legal physician-assisted suicide might so soon be a reality in the United States. However, thanks to two recent rulings by Federal Circuit Courts of Appeals, the legal way for assisted suicide has been paved in 12 states and a precedent probably set for the rest of the country as well.

The first of these rulings, *Compassion in Dying v. State of Washington*, came in March 1996 out of the Ninth Circuit Court located in San Francisco, which covers nine Western states. The ruling struck down a Washington State law banning physician-assisted suicide. Only a month later, the Second Circuit Court, which covers Connecticut, New York and Vermont, rendered a similar ruling in *Quill v. Vacco*, shooting down a New York anti-assisted-suicide law. Of all the states covered by these decisions, Oregon stands to be the most quickly affected, as it previously passed the Death With Dignity Act (November 1994), by a 52 percent to 48 percent margin, allowing physicians who follow certain guidelines to prescribe a lethal dose of medication to terminally ill patients. Only a court injunction now stands in the way of the Oregon law taking effect. The Supreme Court heard the cases in January 1997 and is expected to rule on assisted suicide in summer 1997.

SOME FUNDAMENTAL QUESTIONS

As a young physician just about to finish residency training and enter practice, I find myself forced by these legal decisions to ask some fundamental questions about my profession, primarily about how legal physician-assisted suicide would affect the ethos of medicine. I share my reflections on this question not as an expert in biomedical ethics nor as a legal scholar, but rather as one trying to discern how my profession might change if assisted suicide were to become standard practice.

In my view, the recent court rulings on assisted suicide challenge three basic assumptions about the moral core of medicine as a profession: first, the centrality of the axiom *Primum non nocere* ("First do no harm"); second, the principle of double effect; and third, the moral distinction between actively taking a life and allowing a person to die by choosing not to employ artificial means of life-support.

From practically their first days in medical school, students are taught one of the central tenets of medical practice: "First do no harm." To nonphysicians, such a dictum may sound at least unnecessary, if not ridiculous. But those who have practiced medicine appreciate the awesome power of medical technology for both benefit and harm. The same medications that alleviate suffering can cause horrific side effects. Practically every medication known, even the most seemingly benign over-the-counter remedy like aspirin, has at one time or another caused irreparable damage. Furthermore, who in today's technological world does not recognize the tremendous harmful potential of the machines that can sustain life even in the face of overwhelming disease, when the only alternative is further suffering or unconscious life? With this in mind, physicians must learn restraint, always questioning if a given intervention may cause more harm than good. Assisting in a patient's suicide directly contradicts this life-respecting and humbling assertion that our first duty is to do no harm. It is perhaps the ultimate hubris to assume that physicians can harness the awful power to end life when we so often do harm with our well-intentioned efforts to save life.

THE PRINCIPLE OF DOUBLE EFFECT

A second way that assisted suicide alters the ethos of medicine is by undermining the principle of double effect. This principle has been a cornerstone of Catholic ethical tradition at least since Thomas Aquinas. The church's magisterium has used it routinely in its bioethical arguments. In my professional experience, it also serves as an important guide for action for many physicians, Catholic and non-Catholic alike.

The principle of double effect affirms that an act that has both good and evil consequences is justifiable if it meets all of four conditions: 1) the act itself is either morally good or at least neutral; 2) the person acting intends the good effect and sincerely does not intend the evil effect; 3) the evil effect is not a means to the good effect; and 4) the good effect is proportional to the evil one.

In care for the dying, this principle plays a key role. Certain acts necessary to alleviate suffering, particularly the administration of large doses of narcotics and sedatives, in many cases hasten death. Practically all physicians caring for terminally-ill patients have hastened death by delivering such medications and have felt justified in doing so because of this principle.

Assisted suicide, on the other hand, cannot be justified under the principle of double effect. In assisted suicide, death is the direct, intended result of the act of prescribing the medication, not an unintended by-product. Furthermore, the good of relieving suffering is achieved by means of an evil action, that of assistance in direct killing. With such erosion of double effect, our entire professional role in caring for the dying changes. In practicing assisted suicide, we no longer act primarily as care-givers but rather as arbiters of the value of human life, giving care when the life seems worth it and helping to kill the patient when it does not. The hubris of this position worries me. As physicians, we should commit ourselves to caring for human life, not to deciding when it no longer merits care.

KILLING VS. ALLOWING TO DIE

Assisted suicide alters the ethos of medicine in a third way by blurring the distinction between withdrawal of artificial life-support and active killing. Both recent court rulings explicitly argued against such a distinction. In the words of the Second Circuit Court opinion, "Physicians do not fulfill the role of 'killer' by prescribing drugs to hasten death any more than they do by disconnecting life-support systems." I find this line of argument astounding. It is one thing to say that assisted suicide is morally acceptable on its own grounds. These courts, however, have argued that assisted suicide is morally equivalent to allowing a patient to die from his or her disease by discontinuing life support when such support can only prolong the dying process. This reasoning not only defies logic but also ignores the ultimate reality of patient care: Every human being dies. Withdrawing life support simply recognizes that the point has been reached when we as care-givers can no longer preserve a meaningful life for our patient, at least not without disproportionate suffering. Assisted suicide tries to prevent this point from ever being reached, but it does so by means of a moral evil, the active taking of life.

The argument that withdrawal of life support and assisted suicide are morally equivalent shows, more than anything else in these opinions, how far short the courts' understanding falls from the realities of bedside medicine. I have participated a number of times in withdrawal of life support when the conclusion was reached that this support could only prolong the dying process. In no sense did I ever feel as if I were killing the patient. Rather, the disease process had progressed to the point where it was going to take the patient's life no matter what we as physicians did or where further life-sustaining therapy would be unduly burdensome for the patient. Turning off a ventilator and thus allowing a patient to die simply does not feel like killing. It feels like, and indeed is, submitting to the natural course of life.

Catholic moral teaching has been particularly clear on this point. Traditional church statements relied on the distinction between "ordinary" and "extraordinary" means, and the latter were considered optional. Recent comments have moved away from the ordinary/extraordinary distinction, perhaps because of its vagueness in light of current medical technology, but have confirmed the underlying tenet that biologic life need not be preserved when efforts to do so are futile or require overly burdensome treatments. However, such allowing to die has never been equated with the active taking of life. The church has been strong and consistent in its teaching that the withdrawal of artificial life support is morally acceptable, while assisted suicide and active euthanasia are not.

SOME PRACTICAL MATTERS

In addition to the three principled objections outlined above, some serious practical matters stand in the way of assisted suicide. First, prescribing a lethal dose of medication for a patient may be much more difficult than it sounds. After the Oregon assisted-suicide law passed, a Dutch physician stated in an interview with *The Oregonian* newspaper that he has participated in over 100 assisted-suicide cases and that in about 25 percent of them, the patient did not die from the prescribed overdose within hours or even days, at which point the physician administered a lethal injection to kill the patient. The Hemlock Society, a pro-euthanasia and assisted-suicide group, acknowledges as much in its literature when it suggests that in addition to taking the recommended overdose, patients attempting assisted suicide should secure a plastic bag over their head to insure death. Both recent Circuit Court rulings do, however, forbid direct euthanasia (such as by lethal injection), thus raising the question of what is to be done when a suicide attempt fails. This practical problem opens the door to the very likely possibility of patients lingering in vegetative states after failed suicide attempts, for whom it would be illegal to give a lethal injection.

A MATTER OF CONVENIENCE

Another practical consideration for assisted suicide involves the "slippery slope" argument. That is to say, while the present rulings clearly state that assisted suicide is legal only for terminally ill patients (explicitly those having less than six months to live), will the practice extend to other people who are not terminally ill? For example, what of those who suffer from chronic, painful diseases that are not imminently life-threatening? And what of children born with malformations or diseases that may require a lifetime of care and perhaps involve much suffering? Most terrifying of all is the possibility that the aged or chronically ill will be convinced by others that their lives are no longer worth living. This possibility of coercion should not be overlooked. Ultimately, I fear that assisted suicide could become a matter of convenience for society, ridding us of our burden to care for the sick and helpless, precisely those who most merit our caring.

Stayskal. Reprinted by permission: Tribune Media Services.

A third practical argument against assisted suicide involves the dismal state of terminal care in the United States. Study after study has shown that physicians regularly ignore their patients' wishes about end-of-life medical interventions. The most recent confirmation of this fact came from the SUPPORT study published in *The Journal of the American Medical Association* in November 1995. This project demonstrated that in five well-respected teaching hospitals, almost half the treating physicians did not know when their patients wished to avoid C.P.R., should they require it; four out of ten patients who died spent at least 10 days in an intensive care unit prior to death; and, perhaps worst of all, half the conscious patients who died were thought by family members to have suffered moderate to severe pain for over half the time of their hospitalization. These dismal statistics reflect the difficulty that modern hospitals have in switching modes from care aimed at cure to care aimed at a comfortable death. They also reflect the nearly complete lack of training that

American physicians receive in managing the dying process. Having just come through medical school and residency training, I can attest to how poorly qualified I feel to help patients die comfortably and well.

Should one wish to remain out of a hospital as death approaches, options may be severely limited. Hospice services can be expensive and difficult to find. Insurance may not cover hospice care (even though hospitalization is much more expensive). And most American physicians do not have the expertise to manage a comfortable and dignified death for their patients. In contrast to ours, the British medical community has taken more seriously their care for the dying. Palliative care is a certified medical specialty in Britain so that well-trained physicians can be consulted to aid in end-of-life care. The hospice system in Britain is also much more developed and accessible to dying patients.

To Give Care Always

Given this sad state of terminal care in our country, if we truly cared about the suffering of the terminally ill, we would work to improve end-of-life care. We would train our physicians properly in managing death, make hospice care available to all who need it, and rein in the aggressive cure-oriented care that our hospitals seem incapable of not pursuing. In the face of these gross deficiencies in terminal care, assisted suicide can be seen for what it is: a simplistic "quick fix" solution to a deeply complex and systemic problem. Practically speaking, I fear that assisted suicide will serve as another excuse not to provide the care that the terminally ill deserve from our society. To put it more bluntly, why care for the dying when they could just kill themselves and relieve us of the burden?

I know that death is not easy either for the dying or for their care-givers. I have seen enough in both my professional and personal life to know that the beautiful deathbed scene of the movies, with its perfect lucidity and freedom from pain, is rare, at best. And having recently helped care for my own mother through her terminal illness, I am deeply aware of the pain of watching a loved one suffer and of the indignities that the end of life can bring. But despite all these realities, I cannot help but view the move toward assisted suicide as both a change in the fundamental ethos of my profession and an abdication of our responsibility to care for the dying. No matter what the courts have said or will say, we who practice medicine should stand by the central moral tenets of our profession: to do no harm, to value life as an intrinsic good and to give care always.

"Unless we make our wishes known,
... life and death become painful
and burdensome legal issues for
family, friends, and doctors."

ADVANCE DIRECTIVES PROTECT THE RIGHT TO DIE

Laura Taxel

In the following viewpoint, Laura Taxel describes the two types of advance directive: the living will and the durable power of attorney. She argues that because doctors often perform unwanted extraordinary lifesaving measures, patients should make their wishes about such procedures known. Signing a living will and appointing a proxy can protect a patient's right to die, she contends. Taxel is a freelance writer in Cleveland Heights, Ohio.

As you read, consider the following questions:

1. According to Taxel, what does a living will allow people to do?
2. Why are family members often prevented from making treatment decisions for the dying, according to the author?

Excerpted with permission from "Defending Your Right to Die" by Laura Taxel, Natural Health, May/June 1994. For a trial issue of Natural Health, call 1-800-526-8440.

Thirteen years ago, Jeanne Dooley's mother was diagnosed with terminal lung cancer. "No one in the family, not even my mother, was aware of what we'd be facing at the end. When she could no longer speak, I had no idea whether she would have wanted to be medicated and comfortable, or placed on breathing equipment that could prolong her life but also her pain. I had to make those choices, and even now I still wonder if I did the right thing. I wish I had known what she would have wanted."

Dooley, a social worker and program specialist for the American Association of Retired Persons, leads workshops to show people how to prepare for such a time themselves. She's quick to point out, however, that "this is not an issue that concerns just the elderly. I could walk out of here today, be hit by a bus, and end up in a coma. It's horrible to contemplate, but it happens."

Two Different Kinds of Advance Directive

In her workshops, Dooley explains the need for preparing a legally enforceable document called an advance medical directive. *Advance directive* is a general term that refers to two separate documents: a *living will* and a *durable power of attorney for health care*.

A living will lets you record your wishes about life support; it's essentially a detailed guide for your family and doctors to follow in the event that you are unable to express your wishes. When the United States Supreme Court sanctioned the use of living wills in 1990, many people thought it was enough to prepare a simple document stating that no "heroic measures" be taken to prolong their life. But the issues surrounding the artificial prolongation of life—even the definition of death itself—are quite complex.

Some experts believe that detailed living wills with precise instructions are a surer way to protect your rights, because doctors are more likely to abide by specific instructions than broad guidelines. Other experts believe that detailed instructions only create ambiguity. In September 1993, *Consumer Reports* published a form that allows people to make specific choices about treatment under six different medical conditions. The form, which a person attaches to his or her standard medical directive, is intended to avoid ambiguity in medical decisions by outlining specific circumstances. In filling out the form, for example, you would check one of three boxes regarding your decision to have artificial feeding in the event that you were in a coma and had an "uncertain chance of regaining awareness and higher mental functioning": "I want," "I do not want," or "I want a trial; if no

Last rights

ROTHCO

© Adair/Rothco. Reprinted by permission.

clear improvement, stop treatment."

Yet the form, although clever and simple, is far from perfect. "The sample form published by *Consumer Reports* is problematic because the people who created it didn't understand the laws that govern medical practice and patient rights," says Ann Fade, director of legal services at Choice in Dying, a national organization that helps people plan to die according to their values and desires. "The result is that people are not getting their advance directives honored." Instead of using this form, Fade recommends that people consult a physician before documenting their preferred treatment under various circumstances.

APPOINTING A HEALTH-CARE AGENT

The other half of the advance directive is the durable power of attorney for health care, sometimes called a "proxy designation." The durable power of attorney for health care lets you appoint someone as your "agent" or "proxy" to speak for you in the event that you cannot make decisions about your care. This surrogate, who may be a lawyer but does not have to be, will interpret your living will for doctors if there is any uncertainty about your wishes. In order for proxies to be effective, it is important that you fully discuss your views with them; the better they understand your end-of-life wishes, the more likely they are to ensure that these wishes are honored.

Many people think that a proxy is unnecessary because they

assume that family members can speak for them. Yet many state laws do not permit family members to make these kinds of decisions. And even in states where these decisions are permitted, it is frequently the case that family members cannot agree on steps to take, or find making medical decisions an impossible emotional burden. Others believe that end-of-life choices fall within a doctor's province. But doctors are trained to maintain life, at all costs, regardless of whether it's the kind of life the patient would want. In addition, doctors must practice "defensive medicine," protecting themselves from liability and accusations of neglect.

Advance directives are valid as soon as they're signed, dated, and witnessed by two unrelated adults who are not beneficiaries of your estate. Discuss the contents with your personal physician and have a photocopy included in your medical records. Keep the original accessible with your other important papers, and if you have an attorney, a copy should be in his or her files. You can create such documents yourself—it is not essential to involve a lawyer—and you can make changes in your instructions at any time (changes, of course, must also be witnessed). Standard forms are self-explanatory, but you may find advice from a lawyer, a health-care provider, or a social worker helpful. In order to have your advance directive honored, it's important to obtain the current documents that meet your state's legal requirements.

"Unless we make our wishes known," explains T. Patrick Hill, education director for Choice in Dying, "life and death become painful and burdensome legal issues for family, friends, and doctors. Yet only 5 to 10 percent of the population has advance directives, which express their treatment preferences."

"The health-care advance directive is so broadly written that it may lead to being starved to death in circumstances when you could survive indefinitely."

ADVANCE DIRECTIVES MAY NOT PROTECT THE RIGHT TO LIVE

Burke Balch

Many people sign living wills out of fear that they will be kept alive by machines when they are no longer able to express a wish to be allowed to die, Burke Balch asserts in the following viewpoint. However, he contends, many doctors now presume that patients would prefer to die rather than be kept alive. He argues that living wills fail to protect those who wish to receive lifesaving treatments. Balch is the director of the National Right to Life Committee's Department of Medical Ethics.

As you read, consider the following questions:

1. According to Balch, what is modern medicine's presumption about lifesaving measures and the disabled?
2. What is the most significant problem with appointing an agent to make health-care decisions, in Balch's view?

From "Life and Death Agreements: The Will to Live" by Burke Balch. This article appeared in the February 1996 issue and is reprinted with permission from the *World & I*, a publication of The Washington Times Corporation; copyright ©1996.

A car accident leaves you fighting for your life, with severe injuries including brain damage that makes it impossible for you to communicate with your physicians. Will you be given lifesaving medical treatment?

Your grandmother, enfeebled, has a mind that frequently wanders. Will her nursing home provide her assistance in feeding?

Many people who do not want what they see as a lot of medical technology prolonging the last few hours or days of their life when they are terminally ill sign living wills—and will be tempted to sign the new health-care advance directive. They should be aware that if they do so, they may be rejecting treatment in a much broader range of circumstances than they intended.

The health-care advance directive does allow one to add a "directive about end-of-life treatment in my own words," or to check a directive to receive treatment stating unequivocally, "I want my life to be prolonged as long as possible." However, most who sign it will be drawn to elect either "no specific instructions," leaving all decisions to a surrogate, or the directive to withhold or withdraw treatment.

WITHHOLDING OR WITHDRAWING TREATMENT

The directive to withhold or withdraw treatment is an extraordinary one. It makes no mention at all of terminal illness, the situation most people have in mind when they think about rejecting treatment. Instead, it states, "I do not want to receive treatment, including nutrition and hydration, when the treatment will not give me a *meaningful quality of life*."

This directive is as broad as it is undefined.

By its terms it prohibits both *all* medical treatment (apparently including painkillers and even simple antibiotics) and *all* food and fluids (reaching beyond tube feeding and other forms of assisted feeding to encompass any method of feeding or giving fluids whatsoever).

"Meaningful quality of life" is undefined, although specific examples that the signer can check describe various degrees of mental disability.

How is that likely to be interpreted? Sadly, many today consider virtually any degree of disability to make life not worth living. Disability rights activists are, of course, outraged at such devaluing of life with a disability. They recognize that what most diminishes the quality of life of a person with a disability is not so much the physical or mental impairment as the prejudiced attitudes and actions of too many of the nondisabled, who typically shun, patronize, or pity people with disabilities.

But those who do not themselves share the widespread prejudice against life with a disability should be aware that the phrase "meaningful quality of life" may well be interpreted by those who do. Indeed, in much of modern medicine the presumption is that lifesaving measures are more likely to be denied than to be provided anyone deemed to have a permanent disability.

EXTRAORDINARY MEASURES ARE MOST OFTEN DENIED

Most of the cases that have reached the courts have concluded that the patient's best interests are served by cutting off life support. In fact, according to a survey of doctors published in the July/August 1991 *Journal of General Internal Medicine*, one in three doctors believed that "regardless of the patient's treatment preferences," doctors should be able to decide whether or not to give cardiopulmonary resuscitation for patients "who suffer from severe chronic illness or terminal disease."

A nursing home study in the March 1991 *New England Journal of Medicine* found in over two-thirds of the cases in which advance directives were not followed by the nursing home and medical staff, the patients were denied treatment they had requested. Nearly 1 in 5 patients with advance directives were denied lifesaving treatment they said they wanted. By contrast, in only 7 percent of cases was treatment provided against the wishes of the patients as expressed in their advance directives.

ADVANCE DIRECTIVES PROMOTE AMBIVALENCE TOWARD THE DYING

A living will lets others off the hook too easily. Patients who are unable to make decisions for themselves because, for example, they are severely demented or permanently unconscious have, in a sense, become "strangers" to the rest of us. We see in them what we may one day be, they make us uneasy, and we react with ambivalence. No matter how devoted our care, our uneasiness with a loved one who has become a stranger to us may prompt us to do less than we ought to sustain her life.

Gilbert Meilaender, *Christian Century*, September 11–18, 1996.

With significant evidence that a growing number of healthcare providers are inclined to deny lifesaving treatment even against the express wishes of patients, the greater danger of ambiguous instructions being interpreted in a manner most likely to deny treatment should be clear. Indeed, in this climate of opinion, any individual who would *ever* want lifesaving treatment under even some conditions of disability should certainly steer clear of signing so broad a death warrant as the directive to withhold or withdraw treatment in the health-care advance directive can be interpreted to be.

THE DANGERS OF ADVANCE DIRECTIVES

Some might be tempted to take solace in the notion that whatever one signs will be interpreted by the trusted "agent"— perhaps a family member or close friend—appointed to make the actual health-care decisions. But the appointed agent might die or be unavailable when needed, and a court could then appoint a successor agent who did not fully know and share the understanding and purposes of the signer. (Listing alternate agents can alleviate but not eliminate this danger, because it is, of course, possible that all the alternate agents named could be unavailable.)

There is an even more significant problem. Given the prevailing sentiment against giving lifesaving treatment to patients with permanent disabilities, a health-care agent trying to direct that treatment be provided may well be subjected to extreme pressure from doctors and others to consent to denial of treatment. The vaguer the instructions, the harder it will be for the agent to resist these pressures.

In some cases, health-care providers may even go to court and argue that the agent is being unreasonably strict in interpreting the general language of the instructions. (As there have been a number of cases in which health-care providers have tried to get court authorization to deny treatment against the clearly expressed wishes of the patient, this is far from unlikely.)

THE WILL TO LIVE

There is an alternative. The National Right to Life Committee has prepared an advance directive form we call the Will to Live. Currently obtainable in about 20 states, it will eventually be available in the proper legal form in all of them. Like the health-care advance directive, the Will to Live allows the signer to appoint a health-care agent with authority to make treatment decisions when the signer cannot do so, and it allows the signer to spell out circumstances in which he wishes to receive or decline lifesaving medical treatment.

Unlike the health-care advance directive, the Will to Live starts with a presumption in favor of treatment, then allows the signer to specify *carefully defined* circumstances in which particular treatments should be rejected.

Everyone should have an advance directive to facilitate health-care decision making when one is incapable of making decisions. But the health-care advance directive is so broadly written that it may lead to being starved to death in circumstances when you could survive indefinitely with what you might deem a very tolerable disability. Avoid it.

PERIODICAL BIBLIOGRAPHY

The following articles have been selected to supplement the diverse views presented in this chapter. Addresses are provided for periodicals not indexed in the Readers' Guide to Periodical Literature, the Alternative Press Index, the Social Sciences Index, or the Index to Legal Periodicals and Books.

Peter J. Bernardi	"The Hidden Engines of the Suicide Rights Movement," America, May 6, 1995.
Rand Richards Cooper	"The Dignity of Helplessness," Commonweal, October 25, 1996.
Ronald Dworkin	"Sex, Death, and the Courts," New York Review of Books, August 8, 1996.
Garrett Epps	"Judges Who Support the Right to Die," U.S. News & World Report, January 13, 1997.
Vincent J. Genovesi	"To Suffer and Die in Christ," America, March 23, 1996.
Robert P. George and William C. Porth Jr.	"Death, Be Not Proud," National Review, June 26, 1995.
Steve Hallock	"Physician-Assisted Suicide: 'Slippery Slope' or Civil Right?" Humanist, July/August 1996.
David Heim	"Being Creatures: Faith and Assisted Suicide," Christian Century, July 17–24, 1996.
Richard M. Huber	"A Codicil to My Living Will," USA Today, January 1996.
Stephen Jamison	"Dead Right," Nation, April 29, 1996.
Jack Kevorkian	"My Obsession with Life: An Interview with Jack Kevorkian," interviewed by Jack Lessenberry, New Perspectives Quarterly, Winter 1994.
Charles Krauthammer	"First and Last, Do Not Harm: Allowing Doctors to Aid People in Committing Suicide Is Unconscionable," Time, April 15, 1996.
Eric Lindblom	"Where There's a Living Will . . .," Washington Monthly, November 1995.
Thomas A. Shannon	"Physician-Assisted Suicide: Ten Questions," Commonweal, June 1, 1996.
Andrew Solomon	"A Death of One's Own," New Yorker, May 22, 1995.
Ernest van den Haag	"Make Mine Hemlock," National Review, June 12, 1995.
Allen Verhey	"Choosing Death: The Ethics of Assisted Suicide," Christian Century, July 17–24, 1996.
Wendy Murray Zoba	"How We Die," Christianity Today, April 8, 1996.

CHAPTER 3

HOW CAN PEOPLE COPE WITH DEATH?

CHAPTER PREFACE

Until the middle of the twentieth century, lavish and costly burials—complete with ornate coffins and elaborate grave markers—were the American ideal in funeral rites. Mid-century critics, including Jessica Mitford, author of *The American Way of Death*, disparaged such funeral practices, arguing among other things that interment was unnecessarily expensive and that it used up precious land resources. Perhaps as a result of such criticism, funeral industry experts say that today cremation is rapidly replacing burial as the preferred method for disposing of the dead. In 1996, about 22 percent of the dead in America, and in some states as many as half, were cremated instead of buried.

For some scholars, the switch from burial to cremation signals an ominous trend in American society. Richard T. Gill, author of *Posterity Lost: Progress, Ideology, and the Decline of the American Family*, argues that the decline in memorialization of the dead reflects Americans' overweening interest in their own well-being and a lack of concern for past and future generations. "Our current lack of interest in the dead is related to our increasing lack of interest in the welfare of children," writes Gill. He concludes that proper memorialization through the rituals of burial is a sign of respect not only for the dead but for the living as well.

But funeral industry organizations, including the Funeral and Memorial Societies of America (FAMSA), promote cremation as an option that broadens the possible ways of memorializing the dead. Within the funeral industry, new companies have formed that will launch the cremated remains of loved ones into space or that will scatter ashes at sea, on favorite golf courses, and in other nontraditional settings. These companies maintain that even the most unusual ash-scattering services are less expensive than traditional burials. FAMSA recommends that survivors use the money saved to fund a memorial scholarship or other philanthropic endeavor, which can be a more fitting tribute to the departed.

People cope with the death of loved ones in many ways, from ritual expressions of grief at burial or cremation ceremonies to therapy with a professional counselor. In the following chapter, experts and laypersons explore the merits of various ways of coping with grief.

| "Grieving, once a private matter among Americans, has gone public."

GRIEF SHOULD BE SHARED PUBLICLY

Ellen Uzelac

Increasingly, Americans are sharing their grief in support groups, on talk shows, and in the arts, Ellen Uzelac asserts in the following viewpoint. She contends that public displays of mourning—from the AIDS quilt to monuments for victims of violence—are helping people to find innovative ways of dealing with grief, a trend that she believes is healthy. Uzelac is the author of *Lost and Found: A Journey Through Grief.*

As you read, consider the following questions:

1. What are some of the new types of grief recovery support groups described by Uzelac?
2. According to the author, what was one of the earliest contemporary public monuments of mourning?
3. In the opinion of Russell P. Friedman, quoted by Uzelac, how might public displays of grief be harmful rather than beneficial?

Abridged from "The Public Eye of Mourning" by Ellen Uzelac, *Common Boundary,* November/December 1994. Reprinted by permission of the author.

On a warm spring day in 1987, at the age of 31, I woke up a wife and went to sleep a widow. My husband's cancer had come suddenly, insinuating itself into our lives like an unwanted house guest. But before long it was to clutch us in its embrace like the closest of intimates.

Until Jim died, death had kept me at a safe distance. Sadness wasn't anything that kind words and a loving hug couldn't cure. But afterward, as grief fastened itself to me like a second skin, I noticed how people around me would avert their eyes or change the subject, shrinking into their safety zones. One woman referred to Jim so casually he might as well have been a weather pattern passing in the night.

Ours isn't a culture comfortable with mourning, I discovered. Nor was I. The first night after Jim's death, as I slid my body over to his side of the bed, I practiced saying: "My husband is dead. My husband is dead. My husband is dead."

THE AIDS QUILT AND PUBLIC GRIEVING

The same month, in a storefront a few blocks from my house, another kind of grief was given voice. There, San Francisco political activist Cleve Jones organized the NAMES Project Foundation, which created the AIDS Memorial Quilt, a modern-day monument to a nation's grief over that epidemic. The Quilt, now the size of 15 football fields, is one of grief's newest manifestations—part of an emerging set of symbols that have allowed America to mourn.

"Something is percolating in the culture right now," says University of Chicago professor Peter Homans, an author and psychologist who is assembling a group of scholars from across the country to study the contemporary voices of cultural mourning. "There is a heightened sense of importance being assigned to loss."

Grieving, once a private matter among Americans, has gone public. For years, we hid our pain. Now we announce it on our lapels with colored ribbons. Powerful expressions of grief have shown up on stage (the Pulitzer Prize–winning *Angels in America*, Lynn Redgrave's *Shakespeare for My Father*), at the movies (*Shadowlands*), in popular music (Eric Clapton's "Tears in Heaven"), and in the visual arts.

In "About Time," an exhibition of works by people with HIV, artist John Neilson incorporated his torn birth certificate, a hypodermic needle, a blood-spattered test tube, and his semen in a mixed-media piece on display at a Berkeley, California, gallery. "I've had people come up to me in tears," says Neilson. "The reason I did it was to expose the things I felt ashamed of and was concealing. In doing this, I was exploring myself and the layers and layers of pain I've been dealing with. There are a lot of fears I've confronted. I'm much more in contact with my grief. That helps me heal."

In the 1990s, "grief recovery" books have developed into a publishing niche. On television talk shows, celebrities and ordinary people alike share their anguish over experiences ranging from the death of a loved one to the loss of a pet. In Los Angeles, on a community-access program called *Drive-by Agony*, relatives of slain victims mourn their loss in front of a TV camera.

SUPPORT GROUPS FOR THE GRIEVING

Over the last decade, bereavement therapy has evolved into a credentialed specialty, and schools, businesses, and communities routinely call on grief counselors to help students cope with shootings, employees with layoffs, and residents with natural disasters. There are three-day grief-recovery seminars, "recovery jewelry" (fashioned from sobriety chips distributed at Alcoholics Anonymous meetings to mark anniversaries), and a toll-free grief recovery hotline. Grief support groups have sprung up in the smallest towns, helping people deal with everything from the loss of a loved one to the loss of a breast. There is even a support group for circumcised men mourning the loss of their foreskin.

"Loss is so terrible, whatever instrument people choose that is good for them, I will start by applauding," says former Lutheran pastor and author Martin E. Marty, a history and divinity scholar at the University of Chicago. He adds, "To me, the worst pastors in the world are those who know why bad things happen or believe words can compensate for a life."

In my own small community of South Lake Tahoe, California, I frequently see pink ribbons tied to car antennas and the doors of local businesses—reminders of Jaycie Lee Dugard, a young girl snatched from a street here in 1991 who hasn't been seen since. Pink was her favorite color.

In a unique expression of mourning, Paul Hrbacek and his estranged wife, Sue, obtained the tree that their 15-year-old son slammed into one night in February 1991. Rory Hrbacek and two classmates were killed in the car wreck. His father and an artist friend have crafted from the tree a memorial to fallen children, which will be erected on Lake Tahoe marshlands. The monument will include a plaque that reads: "Say not in grief that they are no more but in thankfulness that they were."

Ultimately, grief is a solitary exercise. It zigzags, climbs, descends, pulls, and pushes. America is not a country that has ever indulged grief, but a combination of factors including the AIDS epidemic, the aging of the Baby Boom generation, pervasive violence, the self-help movement, and rising multiculturalism appears to be triggering changes.

"In America, there is a tradition, almost a truism, that part of our national identity is to be progressive and forward-looking," says Homans, whose 1989 book, The Ability to Mourn, traces the origins of psychology to personal, political, and religious losses experienced by Sigmund Freud, Carl Jung and their colleagues. Americans "are accustomed to not looking back—and now that we've begun to do so, we don't like what we see," he says, referring to societal ills ranging from slavery and racism to the Vietnam War and the AIDS epidemic. "There is an emerging preoccupation in our society, at the social and cultural levels, with the human experience of loss."

Perhaps the earliest benchmark in contemporary America's "cultural mourning," as Homans calls it, is the Vietnam Veterans Memorial, dedicated in 1982. Like the AIDS Quilt, architect Maya Lin's memorial has become a national symbol of mourning. Secular yet spiritual, its two walls of polished black granite create a sense of gentle enclosure for private contemplation within a public space. More recently, survivors of the 1991 Oakland, California, firestorm, which left 5,000 homeless and 25 dead, chronicled their grief on a tile mural hung in a public transit station; Parents of Murdered Children, a support group that has grown to 40,000 members in seven years, has built a traveling Memorial Wall of Homicide Victims; and a children's advocacy group in San Francisco has sewn a white silk Banner of Hope, inscribed with the names of the more than 8,000 children killed in California since 1982.

Public Grieving Bonds the Community

Yet it is through loss that connection comes. "The closest bonds we will ever know are bonds of grief," writes novelist Cormac McCarthy in All the Pretty Horses, which won the 1992 National Book Award for fiction. "The deepest community one of sorrow."

Therapists and clergy suggest that the public expression of grief could help us out of what San Francisco bereavement therapist Darla Romano calls America's "spiritual abyss."

"People are hungry for connection and meaning," says Romano. "If we truly begin to address loss and people dying in a more significant way, then we begin to explore the meaning of life: 'What is the spirit of life? Are there souls? What do I believe in, and how do I celebrate that in my life?' The minute you start asking those sorts of questions, you're into the spiritual realm of meaning.". . .

PUBLIC GRIEVING AND PRIVATE LOSSES

I didn't attend a funeral until I was in my late 20s, and it was for a man I didn't even know. He was a state senator from Maryland, and I was covering the funeral for a newspaper. Standing in the cold rain and watching the faces of his family, I could not stop crying. I think I cried for every sadness I'd ever known. Since then, the losses have mounted: My husband died; two friends have been murdered; an elderly man with whom I was friendly died in his sleep; a favorite aunt died in her early 60s of lung disease, followed a few months later by my grandmother; a close friend now has AIDS; and my mother, who is 60, is battling cancer.

It is difficult to listen to one's mother talk about dying. Perhaps with a mother more than anyone else, we hold on to the promise of continuance. But for the Baby Boom generation, the deaths of parents loom like shadows. And I can think of only a few friends or acquaintances who have not been touched in some way by AIDS.

"Grief is one of the emotional states we go through that's bigger than we are—and there are a lot of us going through it, an entire generation," says Alexandra Kennedy, a California psychotherapist who wrote Losing a Parent after her father died in 1988. "Grief is like an organic tide that moves through us. If we don't acknowledge it, it comes out in insidious ways. If we suppress our grief, as we've done in this culture, we back off from life; we deaden. And as a culture, we become wooden. There's a cultural shutting-down."

A PROLIFERATION OF GRIEVING COMMUNITIES

In the past few years, Kennedy says, she has seen groups of mourners come together—people who have lost parents, victims of fires, people with AIDS. In the process, they are creating new cultural icons and rituals—public expressions that mirror their private pain.

"Grief definitely is an experience that makes us feel alone," she says. "It drives us inward, into the underworld. But humans have a need to reach out and touch another human being. These groups create a sense of solidarity. They are an acknowledgment that we aren't alone, although we experience our grief personally. The ribbons and the quilts—these are rituals and representations that bring loss into a bigger context, a community context. These are enactments that link inner expression with outer experience."

On the first anniversary of her father's death, Kennedy lit a candle and danced to a recording of Samuel Barber's Adagio for Strings, Opus 11. "I felt the missing of him, and the emptiness as I moved," she says. "Then I felt life."

Paul Alt, an architect in Evanston, Illinois, has designed the Labyrinth of Remembering for possible placement in the former Utopian settlement in New Harmony, Indiana. The model includes a sculpture garden, tombs, cloisters, and an amphitheater. "It's looking at mourning in a new sense," says Alt, who with psychologist Homans has taught a popular course at the University of Chicago called "Mourning and Monuments." Alt began studying the public representations of grief after two friends died. He also is working on a play about loss, tentatively titled *Life and Lamentation*.

THE AIDS MEMORIAL QUILT

A single 3-foot by 6-foot piece of cloth, made in 1987 to remember the life of a man who died of AIDS, was the beginning of the AIDS Memorial Quilt.

Since then, the Quilt has grown to over 40,000 of these panels [as of 1996], handmade by tens of thousands of individuals from around the world. Each panel is a unique memorial to a friend or family member who has died. The Quilt still grows every day, just as the death toll from AIDS grows every day.

The NAMES Project, National High School Quilt Program brochure, 1996.

"There is a correlation with society's inability to mourn, if you accept architecture as a biography of our cultural beliefs and values," says Alt. "What's happened is a degradation of sacred spaces. Church architecture has become so sterile. It has all the pomp and circumstance of a basketball arena. If nothing triggers the abstract emotion within you, how do you consider the past and contemplate the future? You're not supposed to remember and linger. I want you to remember and linger."

Darla Romano belongs to a painting group that expresses loss through pigment and brush. "There are a lot of ways that our images, our feelings, our beliefs want to be expressed," she says. "Generally, we're a talking society, and that typically is the most common vein we use. For me, it's been a whole new discovery to let the colors of the paint and the brush lead me to paint what I need to paint. I have seen on my paper the losses in my life converging—the sorrow of sunflowers bleeding and an image of the grim reaper carrying a sickle. When it came out of me, I had no idea—I didn't know what I was painting. I hadn't figured it out in my head. I think we can trust there is this deeper place in us that is guiding us. And I have seen it happen on canvases all around me—images of sexual abuse, the loss of a relationship, the threat of illness. I heard one woman say, 'I'm finding my life again. I'm coming back to my self. I'm starting to know who I am.'"

A Play About AIDS

In November 1993, two months after he had been diagnosed with AIDS, my friend Rob and I went to see *Jeffrey*, a so-called "AIDS comedy" playing in San Francisco. I had met Rob in 1987, a month before Jim died. I knew then that Rob was HIV-positive and that his lover of five years had died two years earlier. Of all my friends, it was this new one to whom I turned for support. In a condolence card to me, he had described "the loneliness, the numbness, the fear." I didn't need an interpreter when I was with Rob; we spoke the same language.

Jeffrey is one of the first plays to wrap comedy around AIDS, and as I sat next to Rob that night, I listened for his laughter. A love story, the play centers on an HIV-negative man who is so scared of contracting AIDS that he tries giving up sex.

"It was very strange," Rob told me later. "I was seeing onstage many of the things I was living in my life at the time. I look at the Vietnam Veterans Memorial, the Quilt, *Angels in America*, and *Jeffrey*. Clearly, there's something going on," said Rob. "What I believe is that periods of grief expression follow periods of some decimation in society, usually a war. What war are we commemorating now? It's AIDS. And in terms of larger society . . . there is tremendous concern about violence in America.

"But is it good, or is it window-dressing?" Rob asked. "Does it really mean something, or is this a fad? I personally think it's important, but for a lot of people, public grieving becomes a way of bypassing their genuine private expressions of grief. It's easier to wear a red ribbon on your lapel or to make a panel for the AIDS Quilt than to sit down and deal with your own devastation."

Questioning the Benefits of Public Grieving

At the Grief Recovery Institute in Los Angeles, telephone counselors answer up to 8,000 calls a month on the organization's nationwide toll-free Grief Recovery Helpline. Mainly, they try to help callers with their immediate crises, then direct them to the institute's three-day recovery seminar, priced at $495, and its handbooks.

Russell P. Friedman, executive director of the 11-year-old group, questions the benefit of public expressions of grief. "The publicizing of grief doesn't actually help at all," he says. "It creates the illusion that 'I'm doing something good,' and while quilts are wonderful, they're not therapeutic. I guess I find a little danger in the public expression of grief. The best it can do is make it okay to grieve. That's good, but it has minimal value because it doesn't teach us to complete our grief."

Rather than "share the pain" support groups or activities, Friedman suggests that people join groups that focus on recovery instead of illness. "The people who go to a support group specializing in loss like suicide or murder end up being in an illness group rather than a recovery group," he says. "They're talking every month about the pain they're in, and 10 years later they're in the same pain because it's not guided to a conclusion."

New Rituals of Grief

Not everyone agrees with Friedman's assessment.

"People are looking for community, and they form community around issues such as loss," says Thomas Joseph Hunt, a psychologist who practices in West Laurel, Maryland. "These communities are creating cultural rituals, which are very important to healing. People will mourn in the arms of specific groupings, such as the AIDS Quilt. It represents both a symbol of healing and a quest for healing. We are looking to the culture for guidance and direction on how to proceed in an often silent and at times mysterious process."

John Novotny, a psychotherapist in Breckenridge, Colorado, has known loss. He has been blind since the age of two, and when I spoke with him, he was awaiting word on his mother, who was undergoing surgery the next day for terminal cancer.

"Grief and loss—in some way, we all are shaped by it," said the 36-year-old Novotny, who has raced in world competitions for the U.S. Disabled Cross Country Ski Team. "The AIDS movement, the Elisabeth Kübler-Ross books on death and dying, the self-help movement, and the lessening of the stigma attached to therapy—all of these things have made grief more accessible.

"And members of my generation are beginning to experience mortality as a result of the deaths of their parents. Mortality raises interesting questions about your own theology, issues of faith, your belief systems and values. You begin to stare these things straight in the face, and nobody's ever ready for it to happen—or at least I wasn't. There truly is, in society at the moment, a surge of people dealing with grief."

Grief is not the purview of any single generation. In Chicago, some newspapers have begun to run front-page photographs and biographical sketches of city youths who have been murdered. Architect Paul Alt calls such things "modern-day cemeteries" and "avenues of grief."

"Why do we tolerate the homicide rate?" Alt asks. "What does this say about our value of life? My answer is that we don't examine what life's values are."

Public Grief Is Used for a Good Purpose

At South Lake Tahoe High School, the only high school in the mountain town where I live, students gathered in January 1994 to memorialize 15-year-old Alfonso "Fella" Mejia, allegedly shot and killed by a 21-year-old man over a $10 bet.

Handmade posters, hastily hung around the small campus, implored students: "Support peace in memory of our peer Fella Mejia. Please wear your white ribbons. Stop the violence in our home, our community."

Pointing to her own white ribbon, the boy's mother, speaking at the memorial service, begged youngsters to stop the violence that had led to Fella's death. "South Tahoe belongs to you," said Verna Mejia. "You've got to bring peace and love to our town."

In the days after the murder, students expressed their grief with signs, graffiti, and black sweatshirts imprinted with the youth's name and date of death. Grief had come violently to a young generation, and their forum was public expression.

"People are giving and getting permission to feel and to talk about feelings," says Novotny. "That's what grief work is—you've got to let it wash over you. A client said once, 'Emotions must move through the body like clouds through the sky.' And I believe there are as many ways to grieve as there are things to grieve about."

Novotny, I believe, is right. And, in creating new voices, Americans are learning to speak the language of grief—a language that each of us, eventually, must know.

"It has become a truism that it is best to cry one's grief, speak one's grief, talk one's grief, and that unless one expresses grief, one is not grieving."

GRIEF NEED NOT BE SHARED PUBLICLY

Michael Ventura

In the following viewpoint, Michael Ventura argues that Americans have become increasingly unfamiliar with the process of dying and have not learned from family and neighbors how to mourn properly. As a result, he maintains, most people now believe it is necessary to publicly display their grief. However, he contends, such displays may simply allow people to avoid acceptance of the death of a loved one. Ventura is a syndicated columnist and the author of several fiction and nonfiction books, including the novel The Death of Frank Sinatra.

As you read, consider the following questions:

1. According to Ventura, what were the characteristics of families and communities prior to 1945?
2. How does television distort people's ideas about death, in the author's opinion?
3. What do the Navajo believe is the best approach toward grief, according to Ventura?

Excerpted from "A Primer on Death: Part II—Theories" by Michael Ventura, Family Therapy Networker, January/February 1996. Reprinted by permission of the author.

Technology has killed death. (Death will one day return the favor.) More precisely, technology has killed our sense and knowledge of dying. In the technological society that has become contemporary America and is fast becoming the contemporary world, real death is hidden away while fantasized deaths are available for viewing in dizzying numbers and variety. This has skewed our vision and increased our fear.

DEATH USED TO BE FAMILIAR

Until the Second World War, when antibiotics became available and great advances were made in medical procedures, death was familiar to everyone. Most people died in their homes, not in hospitals or old-age facilities. Lifespans were shorter. (Before the sanitation of the 20th century, they were much shorter, roughly half what they are today.) By the time you reached adult age, you had inevitably seen people dying—people who were part of the fabric of your life, people you knew, family (the death-rate of small children was very high), neighbors and co-workers. You had also seen animals die. There was no ASPCA where animals were "put to sleep." You killed a sick or disabled animal yourself; or if you were a child, your parents did, and you knew about it. Death was as great a mystery as it is now, but dying was not. How people died, and how they faced death, was a common experience—an experience in which a large spectrum of behavior was possible. Which is to say: dying was alive.

In those generations, you weren't tested by death just once or twice; by the time you'd reached 25, you'd observed dying over and over again. The first several dyings you attended, you were guided by people you knew (not strangers) who'd seen it all their lives. You learned from them and in time became familiar with your own range of feelings and behaviors in such situations, and you learned to discipline those feelings and hone that behavior. But now we attend the dying and die ourselves as rank beginners, with all the trepidation and awkwardness of beginners.

How did this happen?

Before 1945, families usually lived within walking distance of each other, and people who worked together often lived in the same neighborhoods or villages and knew one another for years. In that environment, a whole community shared a death, absorbed its impact, helped with its chores, and said a communal goodbye. Suburban life, modern transportation and the dispersion of commercial centers have made this impossible. Families are spread all over the continent and co-workers rarely enter each other's homes. A person who becomes seriously ill is separated even further. The sick, injured and infirm are taken to hospitals, where they die as though in a distant land, an alien environment where the staff speaks a jargon that might as well be a foreign language. Nobody is being cruel, nobody is trying to deny the suffering of the dying or the fact of their death. It is simply not economically feasible for enough family and friends to be on hand to administer the round-the-clock care a deathly ill person requires.

FAMILIES AND FRIENDS CANNOT ALWAYS ATTEND THE DYING

Usually, it is also an economic impossibility for an entire family, much less the people one has worked beside, to gather around a deathbed together—certainly not for enough time to experience the entire process (rather than just the last crisis of the process, which is what usually happens). So it's not uncommon for middle-aged people today never to have seen anyone actually die. The first death they usually witness is the death of a parent (a fact that makes death all the more frightening, and can't help but create an association between death and a child's terror of abandonment).

It must be emphasized: Nobody decided to shunt death off into such a confined and inaccessible place. It was not done because people were heartless or in denial. It was done because we've willy-nilly chosen to earn our livings in such a way that family and friends are so scattered that they can't share the care of the infirm and the dying, and it's too much for only one or two individuals to manage. So a process of life that for thousands of years was handled by people who mattered to each other is now delegated to professionals—strangers. Thus, the process itself has become estranged. Distant. Unknown. And because it is unknown, it is feared in ways that previous generations would not have imagined.

A GLUT OF DEATH ON TV

And our situation is made worse because our common "entertainment," if you insist on calling it that, in large part consists of dramas in which people are killed. Scan your 50 or 100 cable channels at any time of the day or night, and you see actors pretending to be shot, stabbed, strangled, injured, maimed and killed. But these actors are miming these events with stylized and largely sentimental conventions. So the shock of seeing someone actually die is increased, because it's nothing like the thousands of deaths we've seen on screens.

Even when our screens show us footage of people actually

dying, the effect is very much like watching fiction. Starving peasants-of-color in far-off, parched lands, dying or dead, seem to live on another planet. We know they are real, but those people are so removed from any death that is likely to be ours (our poorest, even our homeless, are not as emaciated), and in seconds these dying people disappear from the screen and their places are taken by some well-fed person much like ourselves who's trying to sell us something or make us laugh. Death has shown its face, but we cannot see ourselves in its mirror. Reality has become unreal, has been killed. For such is the power of death, that even reality can die.

Our disorientation, then, is complete.

There's nowhere we can go for the experience that will enable us to encompass the stark magnitude of the event. In this sense, we are worse than beginners. Without being conscious of doing so, we've absorbed a false or diluted experience that undermines our ability to learn and adapt to the real. When we're finally confronted with a dying loved one, how much time, how much heart- and mind-energy, is wasted while we simply get it through our heads that it's actually happening in the way that it's happening?

In such confusion, and with so little opportunity for experience, it is very difficult to reach into ourselves for what it takes to face another's death, much less our own.

HOLDING THE HANDS OF THE DYING

In a culture that has come to define virtually any intensity as trauma, events that were once looked at as the essences of life, events that were once faced as things to be lived and lived with, are now looked at as problems to be solved, dilemmas to be deciphered, wounds to be healed. In some ways, this seems to have been an advance, in some ways not.

The methods of solving, deciphering, comforting and healing are described in literally hundreds, if not thousands, of theories, each theory supposedly requiring difficult practices. But these practices are not really very different from one another. Broken down to essentials, there are basically three officially sanctioned methods:

1. You talk to people (and hold their hands).
2. You give them drugs.
3. You give them drugs and talk.

In the face of death, all three are pretty lame, in and of themselves. At best, the drugs tranquilize and numb people too fragmented and panicked to deal with their own death, or the death of a loved one, in any other way. As for the talk—when facing death, words die. The presence and sound of the speaker may be a concrete comfort, but that is hard to quantify. People sometimes go to therapists at such times because they can't stand being alone with their feelings, and so it seems the essential element they're seeking is company—company that, unlike much of the company of family and friends, doesn't add to the intensity and trauma.

Expressing Grief May Not Be Necessary

In our own society, faddish therapies stress the idea that openly expressing sorrow, anger, or pain is a good thing, and the only means for "dealing with one's feelings honestly." "Holding things in" comes to be seen as deviant.

Yet nowhere has it been convincingly proved that expressing grief has universal therapeutic value. Perhaps more important, this insistence on the requirement to feel and tell represents an ethnocentric standard that can do injustice to persons and groups who cope differently.

Norman Klein, *Psychology Today*, October 1978.

There is nothing to be said against any of this. After all, both of the world's oldest professions (the priesthood and prostitution) are based on the value of impersonal but gracious company in times of unbearable intensity that must, nevertheless, be borne. But to get grandiose about one's theories in the process seems nothing but ego. Death kills theories, too.

Death has the uncanny ability to kill anything that would approach it with less than utter humility.

One of our greater ironies before death today is that even grief itself has become a kind of theory, and so has lost its humility. Our mythology of grief is based on a mythology of growth—a kind of consumer's attitude toward experience that holds that everything, even death, should help one "grow as a person." Other cultures would find this unnatural and would counsel instead a surrender to the inevitable, an acceptance that nothing, not grief, not growth, not even memory, can wake the dead or make up for what's been lost.

Is It Necessary to Grieve Publicly?

It has become a truism that it is best to cry one's grief, speak one's grief, talk one's grief, and that unless one expresses grief, one is not grieving. Certainly, this makes for a more dramatic experience: something concrete and emotional happens, and in this there is supposedly a relief and release that makes grief easier to bear.

But it's also fair to ask: does the expression of grief actually mitigate the pain of the loss? Or is it rather an artificially induced drama that substitutes for, and hides (or drives further into the subconscious), death's grief? When the drama is done, is not the hole left by the dead still there? Are not all the unresolved issues, that can never now hope to be resolved, still present, still gnawing? Or is it best to recognize that tears are tears, grief is grief, but the dead are dead, and there's nothing anyone can do but live on while the pain slowly subsides and life achieves a new balance, a balance that includes the absence of the dead?

I am told that the Navajo, and many other tribal peoples, never mention their dead. Their belief is that the spirits of the dead now have no place in life; and that tears, if cried, should be cried in private. This belief, so different from what is prevalent among us now, worked for them for centuries. That doesn't mean they're "right" or we are "wrong." It simply begs the question whether it is always good to substitute a smaller, manageable drama for the great unmanageable fact of death.

Are we, with our new mythology of grief, simply trying to bring death to life? To, in effect, wake the dead? When the most fruitful posture, in the long run, might simply be to honor death? To accept that life is strong but death is stronger, because life changes and death (to our knowledge) does not? It may be best to accept that no expression of grief can help but be dwarfed by the immense mystery that our loved one has become a part of: death.

"*Arduous as grief work is, it's the only hope for real healing after loss, ultimately offering a chance for emotional growth.*"

GRIEF FOLLOWS A MORE OR LESS PREDICTABLE PATTERN

Nancy Wartik

Nancy Wartik argues in the following viewpoint that mourning consists of a series of phases. People may experience these phases in different intensities and durations, but ultimately the process ends with healing, she asserts. In order to overcome grief, she maintains, people must consciously work through each stage, possibly with the help of support groups or professional counseling. Wartik is a contributing editor at *American Health* magazine.

As you read, consider the following questions:

1. According to Wartik, what are the three stages of grief?
2. What factors may influence the length and course of bereavement, in the author's view?
3. What are some signs listed by the author that a mourner may need professional counseling?

From "Learning to Mourn" by Nancy Wartik, *American Health*, May 1996; ©1996 Nancy Wartik. Reprinted by permission of *American Health*.

When her 37-year-old husband, Brian, was diagnosed with an advanced case of the skin cancer melanoma, Cathy Adams went into shock. Over the next 10 months she lived in continual fear and panic. When Brian died on Christmas Eve, 1992, leaving her with two young children, "I went numb," she says. "In some ways it was a relief, just to know that was the end of it."

Numbness turned to anger, Adams says, "at everyone and everything"—even God. "I tried to go to church once after Brian died, but I had to leave. I kept thinking, 'How can I accept this?'" Real sorrow didn't strike for almost a year. "The first few months, I didn't feel sad. Then it really hit me."

Plagued by money woes, the demands of single parenting and the desertion of friends who couldn't cope with the enormity of her loss, Adams fell into despair. "Putting one foot in front of the other was as much as I could do," she says. "I had days where I'd break down and just cry all day long. Everything looked black."

Eventually her depression was treated with medication, and Adams moved with her children to a town less haunted by old memories. "I'd never have believed I could go through something like this and come out feeling normal, but I do," says Adams, now 40. "No matter how bad something seems, I've learned you can get the strength to go through it. But that's what you have to do—go through. You can't go around, you can't run away; you've got to go through."

GRIEF OFFERS A CHANCE FOR GROWTH

The journey into grief after someone we love has died is a voyage as ancient as human history, and one that most of us will inevitably take. Not every death provokes grief, of course, nor is grief felt only after a death; we mourn many losses over a lifetime. But the pain of bereavement, striking as it does at so many levels—psychological, physical, social—is one of the most taxing experiences we will ever struggle with. In describing the process more than 75 years ago, Sigmund Freud coined the phrase "grief work." Arduous as grief work is, it's the only hope for real healing after loss, ultimately offering a chance for emotional growth.

Yet in a society where the realities of aging and mortality are often denied—"Death," historian Arnold Toynbee once observed, "is un-American"—the subject of grief has largely been shunned. Those who suffer loss are plunged into bereavement with little idea of what to expect and no way to know if their experience is normal. Believing their strong emotions to be unacceptable, they deny grief even to themselves or mourn in silence.

"Unfortunately, Jackie Kennedy became the model for so many of us, with her stalwart behavior" after her husband's assassination, notes psychologist Catherine Sanders. Dr. Sanders, the author of *Surviving Grief and Learning to Live Again*, lost her 17-year-old son in a waterskiing accident. "So often, bereaved people I've talked with have said they truly tried to emulate Mrs. Kennedy and behave very bravely, never breaking down in public, never sharing. But sharing and breaking down are part of grief."

Some experts say mourning has never been harder. "Increased mobility means we're not always living near family when we experience a death," says Dr. Therese A. Rando, clinical director for the Institute for the Study and Treatment of Loss in Warwick, R.I., and the author of *How to Go On Living When Someone You Love Dies*. "Because most people in the U.S. now die in hospitals, we're not as familiar with death to begin with. And there's a decline in religion and in the rituals—wakes, funerals—that are psychologically important for survivors."

THE THREE STAGES OF GRIEF

Grief is not a single emotion, but a series of phases through which a mourner passes. Broadly speaking, there are three. In the first, a person may feel shock, followed by numbness, denial, a dazed sense; he or she may irrationally look for the loved one to return. Such responses serve to cushion the blow of loss until the mind adjusts to reality.

In the next stage, a bereaved person confronts the death. This is the deepest, most intense phase of grief. "Intellectually, we know our loved ones are not coming back," says Sanders, "yet it seems impossible to let them go. We remain in emotional conflict until we can finally release them." The final stage is a time of healing, the point when the griever turns a corner and begins to adjust to life without the departed.

Progression through these stages is rarely neat and orderly. Often they repeat themselves in cycles of diminishing intensity. "Tonight all the hells of young grief have opened again," wrote British author C.S. Lewis in his classic 1961 book, *A Grief Observed*, which chronicled his responses after his wife died of cancer. "[In] grief nothing 'stays put.' One keeps on emerging from a phase, but it always recurs. Round and round. Everything repeats."

Sometimes after a death, people freeze their most disturbing emotions until months or years later. In *Motherless Daughters*, Hope

Edelman tells of thinking she'd overcome the loss of her mother at 17, only to find herself at age 24 prostrate with longing for her. Grief, Edelman writes, is "not linear. It's not predictable. It's anything but smooth and self-contained. . . . Grief goes in cycles, like the seasons, like the moon."

UNIVERSAL ANGER

Throughout the mourning process, a survivor may be besieged by a confusing slew of emotions. Anger is almost universal. "It's much more pronounced in some cases, but there's always a kind of resentment at the person for dying and leaving you alone," says Dr. Calvin Frederick, a medical psychologist at UCLA. Dr. Earl Grollman, the author of *Living When a Loved One Has Died*, adds that most survivors experience guilt: "Very few escape without saying, 'I should have been more loving,' without blaming themselves for something they did or didn't do." People may also feel guilty at experiencing relief after a death—say, following a lingering illness. And anxiety, despair and depression are common emotions.

STAGES OF GRIEF

Often starting with shock and denial, grief is phasic: the response of the body, mind and soul to intolerable pain and despair. Next, grief encompasses a constellation of reactive symptoms including fear, rage, guilt, blame, and the tendency to be self-destructive. This is followed by the return of feelings such as sadness, loneliness, hopelessness, and helplessness. The final phase—in the classic description of grieving by Elisabeth Kübler-Ross and others—is acceptance, relief, resolution, and recovery.

Unfortunately, not all patients walk through the process in sequence. For them, the timing of these phases may be different or out of order, or they may be stuck with particular feelings that are painful and seemingly perpetual. Often these patients present for therapeutic intervention.

Melvin I. Pohl, *Professional Counselor*, October 1996.

Grief can also cause physical symptoms such as insomnia, stomach problems, fatigue or dizziness. Studies have even found higher than normal mortality rates among those who've recently lost a spouse, as well as a link between bereavement and decreased immune function.

And grief may cause people to question their sanity. After his mother died in 1994, President Bill Clinton reported repeatedly picking up a phone to call her, a fairly typical slip. In addition, normal routines may become impossible. "People drive by a red light and can't recall if it means stop or go," says Grollman. "They go to make a bank deposit and forget how. People worry they're going crazy. They're not. It takes time and effort to regain the ability to function more effectively after a loved one dies."

"Friends will say, 'You have to get out more, stay busy.' That's usually the opposite of what the person needs," says Sanders. "They're exhausted and fatigued. They just need someone to stay with them and listen."

Occasionally a griever has a vivid encounter with the deceased. "Some people have visions or hear the voice of the dead person," says Dr. Sidney Zisook, a University of California at San Diego (UCSD) psychiatrist. "They may not want to admit it, for fear it will seem as if they're losing their mind. But is hearing a voice during bereavement a psychotic symptom? Of course you hear the voice of someone you spent 40 years with."

TAKING MOURNING'S MEASURE

Once it was assumed mourning lasted only six months to a year. But such constraints are unrealistic at best, suggesting that those who don't let go quickly enough are maladjusted. "Grief has no timetable," says Grollman. "It's like fingerprints or snowflakes: different for each person. Resolving grief almost always takes longer than people expect. If it's the death of your child, it's the death of your future. If your parent has died, it's the death of your past. With a spouse, the death of the present."

A wide range of factors determines the course of bereavement, including the mourner's ethnic and religious background, the quality of his or her relationship to the deceased, and the role the deceased played in the mourner's life. Age affects the mourning process (though adults need to recognize that children grieve deeply too), as does gender. A 1993 study of bereaved spouses showed widowers to be more disturbed, and for longer, than widows. "Men are more often dependent on wives to provide their emotional support," asserts study author Dr. Leon Levy, chairman of psychology at the University of Maryland in Baltimore County. "A spouse's death is in many respects a greater loss for men."

Certain circumstances prolong mourning. Rando cites seven: the death of a child; sudden death leaving no time to prepare; a death perceived as preventable, as with suicide; a death occurring after a long illness such as cancer; a difficult, ambivalent or overly dependent relationship between the mourner and the deceased; a lack of social support in the griever's life; and a griever's preexisting mental illness (such as depression) or extreme life stresses (such as a divorce or job loss).

A child's death is perhaps the hardest loss a person can suffer. Not only is it an appalling violation of the natural order, but it also leaves most bereaved parents feeling intense guilt at not having better protected their offspring. "It's a pain that only people who have been through can relate to," says Don Fiegel, a Williamsville, N.Y., pharmacist whose daughter Claudia died at age 20, four months after being diagnosed with ovarian cancer. "It's indescribable, a gut-wrenching, soul-tearing pain."

After Claudia died, Fiegel withdrew from his surviving children and his wife. "I kept it all in, sat by myself at night and cried. I had no empathy, no sense of direction. I started to drink quite heavily. I'd come home late, or not until morning. My wife told me in no uncertain terms that I had to stop. But I didn't give a damn. I didn't care about anything." It took more than three years, until Fiegel joined a support group for grieving parents, before his healing process truly began.

"Unfinished business" between the survivor and the deceased can complicate grief. When her father had a fatal heart attack at 56, Diana Willensky, now an Associate Editor at *American Health*, was 24. He and her mother had divorced years earlier. "I'd always been disappointed that my father didn't know me better, that we hadn't been closer," she says, "but I assumed we'd have time to do that in the future. After he died, I realized we'd never have that chance. It was a huge regret, and it made his death even more upsetting."

DEALING WITH THE EMOTIONS

Understandably, many people want a way to fast-forward through grief. Though there are no shortcuts, bereavement is often harder than it needs to be, because people lack knowledge of what they're facing or of how to prepare.

If a death is anticipated, family members or friends should try to speak frankly with the dying person beforehand. "Sometimes when a person is dying, people withdraw," says Dr. Dorothea Lack, a San Francisco psychologist specializing in bereavement. "But if there are things left unsaid or undone and you can bring them to completion, you don't wind up with unresolved doubts and conflicts."

For many people, giving in to their feelings about the death is the hardest aspect of grieving. Men in particular may resist breaking down, and they have fewer outlets for expressing grief.

"If a couple loses a child, people will ask the husband, 'How's your wife?'" says Grollman. "Men have been told that big boys don't cry. So they camouflage grief with alcohol abuse, or it comes out in physical problems like headaches or backaches. They don't feel free to feel."

Yet dealing with the emotions provoked by a death is crucial. Trying to escape from the process will take a heavy toll in the end. "You can try to avoid thinking about the loss, or cut yourself off from your feelings when you do think of it," says Rando. "You can try to minimize the loss or keep yourself so busy you'll never notice it. But all of those things will cost you. If you don't pay now, you're going to pay later."

Funerals and mourning rites, sometimes maligned as superficial or outmoded ceremonies, help catalyze grief. In traditional Judaism, for instance, mourners sit shivah (Hebrew for "seven") for a week, during which they're not supposed to leave home or work or engage in pleasurable activities of any kind. "It's a very sensible, therapeutic device," says Irene Nathan of Chicago, who has survived the deaths of her husband and four siblings. "It's a whole week dedicated to the memory of the departed one. You mourn as much as you can; you just get it out, cry. It's grief at its utmost depths." Experts urge those who are grieving not to give short shrift to memorial ceremonies.

SUPPORT FOR GRIEVERS

Emotional support is also crucial, though friends and relatives aren't always adept at reaching out. They may not realize how long grief can take to resolve. Or they may not perceive a loss as meaningful, though it leaves a great void in the griever's life. Not everyone understands, for instance, how devastating the death of a friend, a newborn child or even a pet can be. "People may denigrate the death of a pet, saying 'It was only an animal,'" says Rando, "but there's evidence that it can hurt as profoundly as losing a family member."

Tragedies such as suicide or the death of a child may dampen support from friends. "Lots of the things said to the bereaved are signals for them not to share how they really feel," says Dr. Dennis Klass, a bereavement specialist who chairs the religion department at Webster University in St. Louis. "When people say 'You're so strong; you're handling this so well,' what they're really saying is 'I don't want to know how bad it is. It scares me.'"

For the bereaved, the best approach is simply to ask family or friends for help. Alternatively, there are support groups addressing specific types of loss, from the death of a sibling to that of a pet. Such groups allow grievers to connect with others who understand exactly what they're going through.

When a griever becomes "stuck" in mourning, a counselor or psychologist specializing in bereavement may be helpful. Signs that mourning has gone awry include physical symptoms (fatigue, aches and pains) in the absence of emotional distress; uncontrollable anger or guilt; heavy use of drugs or alcohol; and extreme social withdrawal or suicidal feelings.

Chronic depression can also signal that a griever is in real trouble. Some degree of depression is normal in mourning, but severe, ongoing mood disorder is not. UCSD's Zisook has found that two months after losing a spouse, one in four people is clinically depressed; many could benefit from professional help. "We've tended not to bother treating depressive illness when it's part of bereavement," notes Zisook. "We've discounted it as just part of grief. That's been destructive to people's recovery. Depression after bereavement needs to be treated as seriously as at any other time."

WHEN THE WORST IS OVER

To those in the midst of it, grief seems endless. But it does pass. "You wake up one morning," says Don Fiegel, "and all of a sudden that specter isn't there. Or you take two steps forward and only one back. That's when you know you're coming around."

Freud saw the goal of grief work as cutting ties to the dead in order to form new bonds. Today psychologists realize that people shouldn't break all connections to someone they've deeply loved. "I've seen people come to support groups," says Klass, "and say, 'I lost a child 40 years ago. People told me to forget about it and move on, but I've remembered that child every day of my life.'"

Such responses are now viewed as appropriate, even beneficial, as long as they don't prevent the person from forming new attachments or interests. "I remember a mother who lost her son to cancer and was trying to stop smoking," Klass notes. "I asked how she was doing, and she said, 'He's helping me quit. Every time I want to reach for a cigarette, I'll think of him and he helps me.'"

Recovery from grief doesn't mean a resumption of life exactly as it was, however. Just as a deep wound leaves a bodily scar, emotional scar tissue is permanent, even when a person has moved on to a new life or love. From time to time over the years, the scar will ache. Yet many people deeply touched by grief change in remarkably positive ways. They develop new empathy for others who suffer loss or learn to deal more effectively with people or situations.

"My father's death taught me that you can't assume you'll have time to make a relationship what you want it to be," says Willensky. "It really pushes me to tackle problems I might not try to deal with otherwise. I didn't have the opportunity to do that with my father, but it's something I have more control over now."

For her part, Cathy Adams says, "I've found I don't feel afraid of things anymore. I know how to handle them. It's not that I feel that nothing can hurt me again; I know lots of things can. But whatever they are, I know that I have the strength to get through them."

"The one thing you have when you're grieving is grief; the rest of us need to acknowledge the importance of that and let it be, not try to make it disappear."

FRIENDS CAN HELP THE GRIEVING PROCESS

Crystal Gromer

In the following viewpoint, Crystal Gromer contends that people are uncomfortable with the grief of others and often do not know what to say to those in mourning. However, she maintains, friends can help those who have lost a loved one simply by acknowledging the importance of their grief. Friends of the bereaved can offer support in a number of ways, argues Gromer, with the understanding that grief can be comforted but not overcome. Gromer is a freelance writer.

As you read, consider the following questions:

1. How do some cultures express and share grief, according to Gromer?
2. According to the author, what are some things that should not be said to mourners?
3. What are some things that should be done for or said to someone in mourning, in the author's view?

From "An Etiquette for Grief" by Crystal Gromer, *Vogue*, March 1996. Reprinted by permission of the author.

On a hot night in July nineteen years ago, my husband, Mark, died. He was 24 years old. He was smart and witty and bright, he had thick brown hair that he pushed off his forehead and that shone auburn and a little gold in the light, and he loved me, of that I have no doubt. In all the pictures I have of him, including the ones with my dog, he looks like he has just said something very funny. We were married for nine and a half months.

At one precise moment, chronicled somewhere on a death certificate, I lost my world, my brain, my geography, my language, although I didn't lose my life, as Mark did. Standing in a world where the distinction between life and death had seemed a thick, certain boundary, I was not prepared, as no one can be. This is not a trip you can pack for. Grief is utterly lonely.

"What can I do?" people asked me. "Thank you," I murmured, not knowing what to say and trying to reassure them. The truth is there is nothing anyone can do. None of us can boss around life and death. We can't do the one longed-for thing: to make the dead person stop being dead. "What can I do?" I asked recently, when out of the blue, the phone rang on a sunny weekday afternoon and the news came of a friend's death. There is a disconcerting gap in being, suddenly, an outsider. Do I call or write? Do I stop by the house? Do I bring flowers? Food? How close a friend am I? Am I intruding?

CULTURAL RITES OF GRIEVING

In other cultures and at other times, we would know what to do: If I were a Thonga woman from South Africa, I could join the other women wailing on the ground; or if I were a Chippewa, I could paint my face black, or just parts of it, depending on the depth of mourning; in other places in the world, I could wear shabby clothes, shave my head, go unclean, believe in ghosts. I could offer the consolation of an afterlife. My Irish Catholic grandmother sat in her kitchen with her holy cards; "God rest her soul," she sighed.

But these are not the rites of our time and our place. Even religious traditions do not help with the social questions: whether to call, what to say, what to avoid saying. Because these questions came early to me, I have spent a good deal of time thinking about them. There is an etiquette of grief we can learn. It is not so much a set of rules as a way of being. It requires accepting a place for sadness, for something that cannot be fixed. Because of this, it runs counter to a set of cultural assumptions that we have to unlearn first.

Americans are inclined to think we can always start over, a legacy of the nineteenth-century belief in the ever-expanding frontier we are entitled to: Like Huck Finn we can always "light out for the Territory." When Alexis de Tocqueville visited the United States in the 1830s, he concluded that "equality of conditions" here bred belief in human perfectibility, in "indefinite faculty for improvement." Self-help books and twelve-step programs and talk shows tell us we can do it! We really can have perfect thighs. We can stop our addictions. We can learn Spanish in five easy lessons, learn to cook with beans. In the same spirit, we tend to treat grief as a condition, something to be fixed quietly, offstage, in somebody's office for 50 minutes a week, with medication. It's as though our model for grief is a bad root canal. First it's terrible, then it gets better, then it's over. The requisite stages achieved, everyone can breathe a collective sigh of relief when the spouse remarries, the partner finds a new partner, the couple has another child: all signals that grief has ended. It could all fit comfortably into a TV movie.

This palliative urge is hard to subdue. None of us wants to see a friend suffer. We want to help. "You should go out," we say, "see a movie, have lunch with a friend, buy some new clothes." It would be more helpful to offer companionship: "Would you like to?" rather than "You should." It's too easy to fall into judgment, especially when friends talk to friends, and sympathy conspires: She should get more exercise; if she just threw herself into work; if she didn't work so hard; she should really try medication, yoga, massage therapy, eight glasses of water a day. She should be over it by now.

TRITE SAYINGS MINIMIZE GRIEF

American optimism, in the context of grief, is simply bad manners. So are clichés. "Time heals all wounds," a friend repeated to me recently at another friend's memorial service, and in the course of the afternoon, more than one mention was made of that great healer Time. But if we really thought about that word *heal*, instead of just digging it out like a dime, we'd know what a terrible process healing is, how hurtful and how uncertain. The results, whenever Time does bring them, aren't always great. If two years after a Rollerblading accident my left thumb has not regained its mobility, then what can be said about the state of my soul after a friend's death, after my husband's?

We try to minimize grief. "At least he didn't suffer," people say. "At least he's not a vegetable." Anytime you hear "at least" come out of your mouth, stop. Creating an imaginative worse scenario doesn't make the real and current one better; it trivial-izes it. "At least you're young," people said to me. "At least you have your life ahead of you." What? I thought, so this doesn't count? Because I'm young? Besides, at 24 I felt ancient; hearing that I had my life ahead of me only reminded me that I had to slog through perhaps 50 years, every single one of them with-out Mark. The language of comfort wants to ameliorate. That's fine if the misfortune is a bad haircut, a lost job. But the one thing you have when you're grieving is grief; the rest of us need to acknowledge the importance of that and let it be, not try to make it disappear.

Just Say Something

The bereaved I've met really want to talk about their loss. Be willing to listen. You don't have to say anything brilliant. Recog-nition of their feelings with statements such as "This must be very hard for you," and caring comments like "I want to listen" and "I feel so sad for you" are helpful. All that person can think about is that their loved one is gone. Remarks like "You can have another baby," "It is for the best" or "It's God's will" don't help.

Betsy Okonski, *Newsweek*, May 6, 1996.

Tone is important. We need to avoid chipper, but we also need to avoid reverential. After Mark died, I felt as if people saw me as a tragic heroine, a young widow. People tended to look at their hands when they talked to me, which they did quietly, almost as if I were a restive animal. They were only trying to be kind, their voices softened to show they understood. But they seemed to be speaking only to their image of me. I felt lonelier for being still myself, a self no one else wanted to know, for knowing would provide a glimpse of how painful grief is, and how ordinary, like water. Like water, it will fall on us all sometime.

Small Gestures Help

An etiquette for grief should tell us more than what not to do; it should tell us what to do as well. We can lend ourselves out. We should go to the funeral or memorial service, no matter how much we don't want to go, in order to swell the ranks, to be one member of a community mourning an irreplaceable person. Several times in the past five or six years, I have been to funerals and have been surprised how few of the person's colleagues are there, as though it weren't an obligation, as though it were enough to read the notice. The church, hall, room—my neighbor's father's memorial service was in an indoor riding arena—should be full of human faces, human sounds. Chances are your individual presence won't be noticed. But together, all the people who attend the ceremony make the ceremony. Your presence represents a part of a life and it becomes a part of a memorial.

When you write a note—you should *write* a note, and never, ever, simply sign a greeting card—don't begin with "Words cannot express"; you're using words, poor and necessary things that they are, so don't use them to express a vague sense of your own grief. Write down a memory of the person who has died as clearly and exactly as you can: This is what you can give, and it is a gift, another picture. It is never too late to do this, so don't allow yourself the excuse that a month has passed, two months, more; write anyway. At my college reunion, a woman I'd never known at school but who knew Mark came up to me to talk—only a minute or two—about her memories of him. Hearing her recollections seventeen years later felt wonderful because often I think Mark is only a phantom. I wonder if he ever existed; I can no longer remember what his voice sounded like or the feel of his hand on my head. Often, I think, we refrain from saying something truly meaningful because we're afraid it will hurt. Of course it hurts. Pain is not the worst thing in the world, and this is the lesson the grieving person lives. Embarrassment is not, either, and that should be the lesson for those of us who would like to help. Evasion is worse. Forgetting is worse.

We can lend our presence at the funeral, we can lend our memories afterward, and we can continue lending ourselves and our services. After Mark died, I remember wishing that people still wore mourning. For most of us, I expect, that calls up only the image of Scarlett O'Hara dancing scandalously in black, the merry widow. But I wished for something that stood between me and the world. Clothes would have worked, so clearly obvious that even from far away, people would know I was in a different state from the rest of the world: Watch out for me! my clothes would announce as both plea and warning. The gas-station attendant and the supermarket clerk wouldn't tell me to have a nice day. The young man who walked down the sidewalk, up the pathway, knocked on the door of my house, and asked me out on a date could have saved his steps and his breath.

THINGS FRIENDS CAN DO OR SAY FOR THE GRIEVING

We don't use markers of mourning: no armbands or wreaths, no black, no jet, no jewelry made from hair. Each one of us can, however, serve as that marker for a friend, navigating the paths through the grocery store, the post office; we can be a kind of Seeing Eye dog and interlocutor; we can mediate the unexpected greetings, meetings. We can be the person who screens the phone calls so that people won't need to wonder whether they should call or not, and won't have the excuse—"I don't want to disturb her"—not to call. We can drive, we can sort through mail, we can show up and help create a structure out of which the day or the night can emerge.

It's harder to know what to say to an acquaintance who is grieving. There's the first day back at work, the chance meeting at the dry cleaner. Sometimes the panic of doing the wrong thing takes hold. But don't scoot down a nearby aisle of the drugstore or walk out another door of the train; don't avoid someone. You've been spotted, no doubt; the memory of that failed moment, however fleeting and unintentional, endures on both sides. You don't have to begin a conversation with "I'm so sorry." You can say quite simply, "I'm so glad to see you" or "I'm so glad to see you out" or "I'm so glad to see you back." That's enough.

I do not have anything good to say of suffering. Comfort is another matter. The giving and receiving of solace, the very vulnerability of opening ourselves to it, despite embarrassment, despite potential rejection, seem to me the most deeply human of activities. These lessons are learned rather than instinctive. They are difficult rather than easy. An etiquette for grief should help us to live with what is hard as well as to share what is heartfelt.

| "I don't recommend this kind of wake for those who have been stingy in affection, but for those who have been profligate, it's just the honor due."

FUNERALS SHOULD CELEBRATE THE LIFE OF THE DECEASED

Michael Lewis and David S. Toolan

In Part I of the following two-part viewpoint, Michael Lewis describes a funeral that commemorated the life of his deceased father-in-law rather than mourning his death. He asserts that this unconventional celebration was more comforting than the formalized displays of grief at traditional funerals. In Part II, David S. Toolan writes about his cousin's wake, in which family and friends gathered to share remembrances of the deceased. A joyous ritual celebration such as this can remind survivors that life goes on, Toolan contends. Lewis is a senior editor of the *New Republic*, a weekly liberal magazine. Toolan is an associate editor of *America*, a weekly magazine of Catholic opinion.

As you read, consider the following questions:

1. According to Lewis, what two beliefs govern what he calls WASP funerals?
2. In Toolan's description, what are the elements of a real Irish wake?

Part I: From "New York Diarist: The Good Funeral" by Michael Lewis, *New Republic*, August 7, 1995; © Michael Lewis. Reprinted by permission of the author. Part II: "Muldoon's Wake" by David S. Toolan, *America*, December 10, 1994. Reprinted with permission.

One consequence of living several thousand miles from the place you grew up and shifting residences every few years is that the people you care for tend to die at a distance. Once a year or so I get a phone call to inform me that someone I had assumed alive and well has suffered a stroke, or shot himself, or neglected to wake up. Upon hearing such news I usually feel a brief but genuine desire to drop whatever I am doing and fly to the funeral.

Then I recall the funerals I have attended. The very word calls to mind dark suits on a hot day and a room full of uneasy people sitting on hard wooden seats pointed in the direction of a spokesman for organized religion, who, in an attempt to make them less uncomfortable, is conjuring up an implausible illusion of an afterlife. The funeral of my imagination, I should say, is a WASP funeral. WASP funerals are governed by two beliefs: that the public display of emotion is embarrassing, and that khakis are inappropriate. When we WASPs meet over a coffin the best that can be hoped for is a stiff exchange and a bit of meaningful eye contact. And so, within a few hours of receiving the news of a friend's death, my urgency subsides and my reasoning commences: It is a long way to go. . . . It's not as if anyone will care . . . he won't even know. Finally: he would have wanted it this way.

Celebrating a Full Life

The first happy exception in a lifetime of ducking funerals came after the death of my father-in-law, Charles H. Bohner. He was a professor of English literature at the University of Delaware, the author of literary biographies of Robert Penn Warren and John Pendleton Kennedy and a novel based on the Lewis and Clark expedition, and the editor of McGraw-Hill's fine anthologies of short stories. I had known him for a little more than a year, most of which he had spent in a losing fight with cancer, but evidently I had become thoroughly attached to him. Upon meeting him, it had taken me about ten seconds to realize that I would not have to pretend to like my father-in-law, and his demise left me with the sense that I had been robbed of a winning ticket in the in-law lottery. Which is not to say I would not have skipped his funeral if I could have. After all, he was a WASP.

The few funeral homes I have seen all have had a faintly patriotic air, perhaps because love of country is a rare emotion that is both "deep" and generally inoffensive. Ours was no different. Big books celebrating the Birth of America lay open on shiny mahogany reading stands beneath portraits of Colonial dames.

The American Colonial motif was punctuated only by tiny tributes to American commerce: window stickers for Mastercard and Visa; a display rack of urns; a case of sales brochures. These last were arranged neatly on a table beside the entrance. Tucked among them was a pamphlet called *Funeral Etiquette*, published by the Ohio Funeral Directors Association. Although it was intended as a primer for funeral-goers of all creeds, its advice pointed unmistakably to a WASP funeral. Here, in fewer than a dozen pages, was the most complete guide ever written to repressing grief, falsifying sentiment and sublimating honest thought. It included, for instance, handy rules for the receiving line. "Simply state something personal about the deceased or how he or she will be remembered from a previous experience," it commanded, "such as 'John enjoyed life'; 'He certainly had a lot of friends'; or 'Ruth always worried about everyone else's problems.'" Alongside this list was another, titled "Inappropriate Remarks": "you can have other children"; "he is better off now"; "only the good die young." ("He still owes me forty bucks" and "Thank God it wasn't me" somehow were omitted.)

There may be some people who are made to feel better by such rules, but I am not one of them. Neither, it emerged, were my in-laws. The minute I saw my brother-in-law, Russell, I sensed that *Funeral Etiquette* was at some risk. He arrived to orchestrate the secular service wearing a blue blazer, khakis and spanking white Keds, and the air of a son celebrating a father's well-lived life rather than a man one needed to feel sorry for. "Did you buy those shoes for the occasion?" one of his friends asked him as he passed through the receiving line, violating the code of conduct and making everyone feel a bit better. A woman who had been informed that she might dress as she pleased arrived in a tight shocking orange mini-dress. *Funeral Etiquette* retired to its place in the rack.

Breaking the Rules of Funeral Etiquette

"A eulogy is uncommon at today's funeral service," whispered the offensive pamphlet from afar. "It is *not* inappropriate, but the eulogy is not to be lengthy, and should offer praise and commendation to the person who has died." While the rest of us sat on soft, comfortable benches, a passionate Castilian painter, apparently ignorant of all rules, rose and described in sordid and lengthy detail his forty-year friendship with a man he could not bring himself to call simply "Charles" and so instead had dubbed with an endless comical rolling "r", ¡*Don Carlos, el más guapo!* (the most handsome, fearless and courageous). When the applause had died down, Don Carlos's three children took turns telling tales of their father—his failures as well as his triumphs—that raised belly laughs from the audience and made the Colonial dames on the walls quake.

After the memorial service the family drove the mortal remains of the author and professor of English literature to the Chesapeake Bay. Scattering a man's ashes in the sea sounds easier than it is. The wind was blowing in, the waves were crashing against the rocks, and everywhere we looked there seemed to be a crowd of middle-aged women in bathing suits. Appropriately, there seemed no appropriate place to put him. Finally, it was decided that the best strategy was to climb down a sea wall and discreetly heave the makeshift urn into the Bay. I stood on a slippery rock and pried the lid off the large golden tin while Russell found his footing at the water's edge. I had never before seen human ashes. They aren't at all like what you find at the bottom of the fireplace on a winter morning. They are pulverized gray stones, heavy and flecked with pieces of white. Still they rose in a white puff, as the canister sank, and formed man-shaped patterns on the surface of the bay.

II

My father used to talk of them, of course—they were the only occasions, he would say, on which the poor Irish immigrants of his youth had splurged and held a party—but until recently the closest I had ever come to participating in a genuine Irish wake was at the death of a Quaker. I owe my rediscovery of this almost forgotten tradition to my first cousin, Dennis Muldoon—whom I'd always rated the best hugger in my extended family. He accidentally stepped off a mountain and plunged 600 feet to his death. On a business trip to Arizona, he had taken a day off to hike up Oak Creek Canyon outside of Sedona. It had snowed the night before, the Park Rangers told us, and the footing was slippery, or the friend's dog he had with him tugged and caught him off balance. It's futile to speculate how it happened, but somehow one wants to recapture those final moments. The horror eats at you. When my brother's commuter plane crashed into New York harbor, I'd replayed his death in my tortured, sleepless imagination for months on end. Dennis was only 45—and left a lovely wife and three children, the youngest son only in first year high school.

From all across the country—Boston, Washington, D.C., Chicago and the West Coast—the clan gathered, in shock, for the funeral in Dallas, Texas. Thank God for big families: a widowed mother, seven siblings and their spouses, lots of nephews and nieces, his wife Kathy's parents and her three brothers and a sister, first cousins like me. And more, of course—neighbors, business friends and friends of the children. We were only later to find out what those young people meant.

R.J. DURSLAG
"I'D RATHER BE LIVING"

SCHWADRON

. © Harley Schwadron. Reprinted by permission.

Like many big, assimilated Irish-Catholic families, various members of the Muldoon tribe have pursued their spiritual quests far afield—and hence any family reunion these days is necessarily interreligious, as likely to involve sacred crystals and Buddhist mantras as the Bible and rosaries. But none of them has lost their inherited sacramental sense; instinctively, they know how to ritualize an event, be it of sorrow or joy, and some of my most electric experiences of forgiveness and reconciliation have occurred in a Muldoon home.

A FUNERAL IS A CELEBRATION

For instance, even as their father lay dying of cancer, my cousins had finagled an early coffin (said it was for a school play), which they placed in their parents' garage and then proceeded to paint, each son and daughter and grandchild figuring the story of their turbulent relationship with this combative, demanding patriarch in vivid symbol and psychedelic color. At the funeral Mass, the brilliant coffin—and the truth-telling poetry that had spilled out of these very verbal sons and daughters—had created something of a parish sensation (some would even say a scandal). And as the pallbearers carried off my uncle's remains to be cremated, my cousins raised high their glasses of Glenlivet, the Old Man's favorite whiskey, and their mother, my mother's sister, shattered the glass she held for her mate of 55 years against the garden wall. The final toast sent my stomach into my throat, yet it was a glorious, Joycean send-off worthy of a Gaelic chieftain—full of yeses.

But the sudden, violent death of a young husband and brother is much harder to take, much less to celebrate, than the death of a father rich in wisdom and years. In fact, the very word "celebrate" grates on the teeth. Official obits, even laudatory ones like the Dallas papers carried, offer little solace. (One of Dennis's last projects, noted the papers, had been to chair the city's nonprofit Trinity Ministry, which serves 100,000 meals a year to the homeless and offers vocational programs, transportation, clothing and other assistance to the poor.) How, then, would my cousins console their brother's family and each other? What would they invent to absorb and transform this numbing shock into a heartening yes? The only thing I was fairly sure about was that there would be no funeral parlor setting for this unruly crowd. And I was right—for after a late afternoon rosary in the austere stone chapel of the local Cistercian abbey, they brought Dennis's bruised body home for a real Irish wake. A big buffet supper. And then, starting about 9 P.M., some 30 or 40 of us, family and friends, sat with the man whose abrupt exit we couldn't yet fathom or accept. His casket stood open in the back sunporch of his own house, and there we remembered him—and ourselves—with poems, stories and testimonies. Weeping and laughing, we went on, spooling out his life, until about 2 in the morning.

REMEMBERING GOOD AND BAD ABOUT THE DECEASED

No one, it seems, had the whole story; each of us held a thread, made a stitch. His sisters and brothers talked directly to him, there in his coffin, in verse dug from the pit of their heartbreak—and reminded us of the fiercely self-reliant kid who often took the punishment a younger brother had earned, who had been in the habit of running away from home and losing himself in the woods (often camping out in mid-winter), who wasn't really the natural athlete I admired but simply one who drove himself harder than his teammates could ("he had a high threshold of pain," as one brother put it). His daughter Moira spoke of how fitting it was that her dad died, as he had lived, in a great open space, on a mountaintop, with a dog at his side (he loved animals); and his son Ryan fondly evoked the rough-house basketball player his soccer-loving father had been ("the idea was to beat me up"). A niece picked up the anger that many of us felt: She railed at him, this uncle who had always been "there for me," for abandoning her so quixotically; and one cousin, for whom this man had been the brother he never had, still shuddered at the memory of a hike in the high Sierras in which Dennis's recklessness had all but turned them into ice fossils. On balance, it was remarkable he had lived so long.

There was no need to drown sorrow in sentimentality. Dennis was a sweet man, but this did not mean he hadn't infuriated us on more than one occasion. It escaped no one that he could be wilful and impetuous. He never lost his boy's wildness and big-dreaming heart, but perhaps because of that he often proved a truculent, bossy business partner and hard on those he loved. "Saint Dennis," his wife gently mocked the next day—"he could be such a lunkhead."

As with all of us, his strengths were his weaknesses. Even so, much will be forgiven the best hugger in the clan. But like many other family members, I'd hardly guessed the breadth of his embrace. It turned out that all those college kids at the wake weren't there just because they were chums of his children; they were there to testify that when they had been troubled teen-agers, unable to talk to their own parents, Dennis had taken them in (both girls and boys, usually putting them to work building a wall or fixing the house) and listened—and listened again. They could pour out their guts to him. His wife (who had a part in this role as well) revealed that whenever she came downstairs in the morning she never knew whom she would find sleeping over on the living room floor—and here many of them were, grieving the loss of their truest adult confidant. And giving thanks for his welcome, his generous ear—and the cigars he passed out so equitably to both girls and boys.

Life Goes On Noisily

Through their tears and laughter, neighbors had reminded us that the perennial big kid in Dennis had often driven them crazy; you could never tell at what day or hour—except that inevitably it was unpredictable and a late one—he would decide to shoot off fireworks from his roof. So what else could we do to close out an awakening to the terrible beauty, the grace of a life that

had so touched us to the quick, but to sing a hymn he loved—
"Amazing Grace"? (For the first time, the context was right; my
cousin had been that.) Then we retreated to the back yard, where
Chris, the youngest son, set off an arsenal, blazoning the dark
night sky with sound and light—a final salute to his father. And a
sign that life, at least in this family, will go on, noisily.

I don't recommend this kind of wake for those who have
been stingy in affection, but for those who have been profligate,
it's just the honor due. In any case, my cousins had recovered for
me something worth preserving—for which I thank them. The
lesson? Let the Master of the Universe catch the fall . . . and
breathe. And as you do, let the full gamut of memory pour in,
and with it the full flood of aching loss. For the ache of memory, what's that except the real presence—like a gigantic power
station—of the one and many who have loved us, whom we
have loved? Dennis was there with us that night in a great company of departed kin, mixing his tears and laughter with ours—
and yes, quickening us, rebirthing us with passion, that great
yea, that moves the stars and awakens the dead.

> "I can remember my father saying that the reason we had funerals and open caskets was so we might confront what he called 'the reality of death'."

FUNERALS SHOULD HELP SURVIVORS TO CONFRONT DEATH

Thomas Lynch

Thomas Lynch is an undertaker in Milford, Michigan, and the author of several books of poetry, including *Grimalkin and Other Poems*. In the following viewpoint, Lynch contends that funerals have always served the purpose of helping the living to confront their own mortality. By forcing survivors to face the prospect of death, he argues, such rituals of paying respect to the deceased can increase respect for life.

As you read, consider the following questions:

1. In Lynch's opinion, what do the bodies of the newly dead represent?
2. According to the author, when did the practice of embalming become prevalent?
3. In the author's view, what are the consequences of considering death to be inconvenient?

From "Embalming Father" by Thomas Lynch, *London Review of Books*, vol. 17, no. 14, July 1995. This article will also appear in Mr. Lynch's forthcoming book *The Undertaking* (W.W. Norton). The article is reprinted here by permission of Thomas Lynch, the *London Review of Books*, and W.W. Norton.

The undertakers are over on the other island. They are there for what is called their Midwinter Conference: the name they give to the week in February every year when funeral directors from Michigan find some warm place in the Lesser Antilles to discuss the pressing issues of their trade. The names for the workshops and seminars are borderline: 'The Future of Funeral Service', 'What Folks Want in a Casket', 'Coping with the Cremation Crowd'—things like that. The resorts must have room service, hot tubs, good beaches and shopping on site or nearby. No doubt it is the same for orthodontists and trial lawyers.

And I'm here on the neighbouring island—a smaller place with a harbour too shallow for cruise ships and no airport. I'm a ferry boat ride from the undertakers from my home state. But I've timed my relief from the Michigan winter with theirs in case I want to register for a meeting and write off my travel. It is legal and sensible and would reduce the ultimate cost of funerals in my town where I am the funeral director and have been for 25 years now.

But I just can't work up any enthusiasm for spending any portion of the fortnight discussing business. It's not that they aren't a great bunch, chatty and amiable as stockbrokers or insurance types; and out of their hometowns, incognito, hell-bent on a good time, they can be downright fun, if a little bingy. It's just that it seems I've been in a Midwinter Conference of my own for a long time now. Enough is enough, I need to walk on the beach now and contemplate my next move.

THE ROLE OF PROFESSIONAL FUNERAL DIRECTORS

My father was a funeral director and three of my five brothers are funeral directors; two of my three sisters work pre-need and bookkeeping in one of the four funeral homes around the metro area that bear our name, our father's name. It is an odd arithmetic—a kind of family farm, working the back forty of the emotional register, our livelihood depending on the deaths of others in the way that medicos depend on sickness, lawyers on crime, the clergy on the fear of God. I can remember my mother and father going off on these Midwinter Conferences and coming back all sunburned and full of ideas and gossip about what my father insisted we call our 'colleagues' rather than the 'competitor'. He said it made us sound like doctors and lawyers, you know, professionals—people you could call in the middle of the night—if there was trouble, people whose being had begun to meld with their doing, who were what they did.

Our thing—who we are, what we do—has always been about death and dying and grief and bereavement: the vulnerable underbelly of the hardier nouns: life, liberty, the pursuit of . . . well, you know. We traffic in leavetakings, goodbyes, final respects. 'The last ones to let you down,' my father would joke with the friends he most trusted. 'Dignified Service' is what he put on the giveaway matchbooks and plastic combs and rainbonnets. And he loved to quote William Ewart Gladstone, a great Victorian Liberal who sounded like a New Age Republican when he wrote that he could measure with mathematical precision a people's respect for the laws of the land by the way they cared for their dead.

Of course, Gladstone inhabited a century and an England in which funerals were public and sex was private and, though the British were robbing the graves of infidels all over the world for the British Museum, they did so, by all accounts, in a mannerly fashion. I think my father first heard about Gladstone at one of these Midwinter Conferences and lately I've been thinking how right they were—Gladstone, my father.

A Father's Death

My father died three years ago tomorrow on an island off the Gulf coast of Florida. He wasn't exactly on a Midwinter Conference. He'd quit going to those years before, after my mother had died. But he was sharing a condo with a woman friend who always overestimated the remedial powers of sexual aerobics. Or maybe she only underestimated the progress of his heart disease. We all knew it was coming. In the first of his widowhood, he sat in his chair, heartsore, waiting for the other shoe to drop. Then he started going out with women. The brothers were glad for him. The sisters rolled their eyes a lot. I think they call these 'gender issues'. In the two years of consortium that followed, he'd had a major—which is to say a chest ripping, down for the counter—heart attack every six months like clockwork. He survived all but one. 'Three out of four,' I can hear him saying, 'you're still dead when it's over.' He'd had enough. Even now I think of that final scene in David Lean's old film when Zhivago's heart is described as 'paper thin'. He thinks he sees Lara turning a corner in Moscow. He struggles to get off the bus, loosens his tie, finally makes it to the sidewalk where, after two steps, he drops dead. Dead chasing love, the thing we would die for. That was my father—stepping not off a bus but out of a shower in his timeshare condo, not in Moscow but on Bocca Grande, but chasing, just as certainly, love. Chasing it to death.

When we got the call from his woman friend, we knew what to do. My brother and I had done the drill in our heads before. We had a travelling kit of embalming supplies: gloves, fluids, needles, odds and ends. We had to explain to the security people at the airlines who scrutinised the contents of the bag, wondering how we might make a bomb out of Dodge Permaglo [embalming fluid] or overpower the cabin crew with a box marked 'Slaughter Surgical Supplies' full of stainless steel oddities they'd never seen before. When we got to the funeral home they had taken him to, taken his body to, the undertaker asked us if we were sure we wanted to do this—our own father after all?—he'd be happy to call in one of his embalmers. We assured him that it would be OK. He showed us into the prep room, that familiar decor of porcelain and tile and fluorescent light—a tidy scientific venue for the witless horror of mortality, how easily we slip from is to isn't.

It was something we had always promised him, though I can't now, for the life of me, remember the context in which it was made—the promise that when he died his sons would embalm him, dress him, pick out a casket, lay him out, prepare the obits, contact the priests, manage the flowers, the casseroles, the wake and procession, the Mass and burial. Maybe it was just understood. His was a funeral he would not have to direct. It was ours to do; and though he'd directed thousands of them, he had never made mention of his own preferences. Whenever he was pressed on the matter he would only say: 'You'll know what to do.' We did.

BODIES ARE NOT JUST SHELLS

There's this 'just a shell' theory of how we ought to relate to dead bodies. You hear a lot of it from young clergy, old family friends, well intentioned in-laws—folks who are unsettled by the fresh grief of others. You hear it when you bring a mother and a father in for the first sight of their dead daughter, killed in a car wreck or left out to rot by some mannish violence. It is proffered as comfort in the teeth of what is a comfortless situation, consolation to the inconsolable. Right between the inhale and exhale of the bonewracking sob such hurts produce, some frightened and well-meaning ignoramus is bound to give out with: 'It's OK, that's not her, it's just a shell.' I once saw an Episcopalian deacon nearly decked by a swift slap from the mother of a teenager, dead of leukaemia, to whom he'd tendered this counsel. 'I'll tell you when she's "just a shell",' the woman said. 'For now and until I tell you otherwise, she's my daughter.' She was asserting the longstanding right of the living to declare the dead dead. Just as we declare the living alive through baptisms, lovers in love by nuptials, funerals are the way we close the gap between the death that happens and the death that matters. It's how we assign meaning to our little remarkable histories.

And the rituals we devise to conduct the living and beloved and the dead from one status to another have less to do with *performance* than with *meaning*. In a world where 'dysfunctional' has become the operative adjective, a body that has ceased to work has, it would seem, few useful applications—its dysfunction more manifest than the sexual and familial forms that fill our tabloids and talk shows. But a body that doesn't work is, in the early going, the evidence we have of a person who has ceased to be. And a person who has ceased to be is as compelling a prospect as it was when the Neanderthal first dug holes for his dead, shaping the questions we still shape in the face of death: 'Is that all there is?' 'What does it mean?' 'Why is it cold?' 'Can it happen to me?'

A Serious Threat

I would argue that the current movement toward lessening, or even abandoning, the memorialization of our dead is a reflection of deeper forces in society, and that these deeper forces, far from being uniformly healthy and benign, may well pose a serious threat to our future national well-being. . . .

I believe that our current lack of interest in the dead is related to our increasing lack of interest in the welfare of children. That is, both reflect a given generation's interest in its own well-being over the course of its own life-span, and a general lack of interest in the future that will be inherited by one's children.

Richard T. Gill, *Public Interest*, Spring 1996.

So to suggest in the early going of grief that the dead body is 'just' anything rings as tinny in its attempt to minimalise as it would if we were to say it was 'just a' bad hair day when the girl went bald from her chemotherapy, or that we hope for heaven on her behalf because Christ raised his 'just a' body from dead. What if rather than crucifixion he'd opted for suffering lowly self-esteem for the remission of sins? What if, rather than 'just a shell', he'd raised his personality, say, or the Idea of Himself? Do you think they'd have changed the calendar for that? Done the Crusades? Burned witches? Easter was a body and blood thing, no symbols, no euphemisms, no half-measures. If he'd raised anything less, of course, as Paul points out, the deacon and several others of us would be out of business or back to Saturday Sabbaths, a sensible diet and no more Christmases.

The bodies of the newly dead are not debris or remnant, nor are they entirely icon or essence. They are, rather, changelings, incubates, hatchlings of a new reality that bear our names and dates, our image and likenesses, as surely in the eyes and ears of our children and grandchildren as did word of our birth in the ears of our parents and their parents. It is wise to treat such new things tenderly, carefully, with honour.

DEATH REMINDS PEOPLE OF THEIR OWN MORTALITY

I had seen my father horizontal before. At the end it had been ICUs mostly, after his coronaries and bypasses. He'd been helpless, done unto. But before that there had been the man stretched out on the living-room floor tossing one or the other of my younger siblings in the air or napping in his office at the first funeral home in full uniform, black three-piece, striped tie, wingtips, clean shave, or in the bath-tub singing 'from the halls of Montezuma to the shores of Tripoli'. He had outbreaks of the malaria he'd gotten in the South Pacific. In my childhood he was, like every father on the block, invincible. That he would die had been a fiction in my childhood, a fear in my twenties, a spectre in my thirties—and, in my forties, a fact. But seeing him, outstretched on the embalming table of the Anderson Mortuary in Ft Myers with the cardiac blue in his ears and fingertips and along his distal regions, shoulders and lower ribs and buttocks and heels, I thought *this is what my father will look like when he's dead.* And then, like a door slammed shut behind you, the tense of it all shifted into the inescapable present of—*this is my father, dead.* My brother and I hugged each other, wept with each other and for each other and for our sisters and brothers, home in Michigan. Then I kissed my father's forehead, not yet a shell. Then we set to work in the way our father had trained us.

He was a co-operative body. Despite the arteriosclerosis, his circulatory system made the embalming easy. And having just stepped from the shower into his doom, he was clean and cleanly shaven. He hadn't been sick, in the hospice or intensive care sense of the word. So there were none of the bruises on him or tubes in him that medical science can inflict and install. He'd gotten the death he wanted, caught in full stride, quick and cleanly after a day strolling the beach picking sea shells for the grandchildren and maybe after a little bone bouncing with his condo-mate, though she never said and we never asked and can only hope. And massaging his legs, his hands, his arms, to effect the proper distribution of fluid and drainage, watching the blue clear from his fingertips and heels as the fluid which would preserve him long enough for us to take our leave of him worked its way around his body, I had the sense that I was doing something for him even though, now dead, he was beyond my kindnesses or anyone's. Likewise, his body bore a kind of history: the tattoo with my mother's name on it he'd had done as an 18-year-old marine during World War Two, the perfectly trimmed moustache I used to watch him darken with my mother's mascara when he was younger than I am and I was younger than my children are. The scars from his quintuple bypass surgery, the AA medallion he never removed and the signet ring my mother gave him for his 40th birthday, all of us saving money in a jar until 50 dollars were accumulated. Also there were the greying chest hairs, the hairless ankles, the male pattern baldness I see on the heads of men in the first-class section of airplanes now and in the double mirrors in the barber's shop. And embalming my father I was reminded of how we bury our dead and then become them. In the end I had to say that maybe *this is what I'm going to look like dead.*

THE LIVING NEED TO BURY THE DEAD

Maybe it was at a Midwinter Conference my father first thought about what he did and why he did it. He always told us that embalming got to be, forgive me, *de rigueur* during the Civil War when, for the first time in our history, lots of people—mostly men, mostly soldiers—were dying far away from home and the families that grieved for them. Dismal traders worked in tents on the edge of battlefields charging, one reckons, what the traffic would bear to disinfect, preserve and 'restore' dead bodies—which is to say they closed mouths, sutured bullet holes, stitched limbs or parts of limbs on and sent the dead back home to wives and mothers, fathers and sons. All of this bother and expense predicated on the notion that the dead need to be at their obsequies, or more correctly that the living need the dead to be there, so that the living can consign them to the field or fire after commending them to God or the gods or Whatever Is Out There. The presence and participation of the dead human body at its funeral is, as my father told it, every bit as important as the bride's being at her wedding, the baby at its baptism.

And so we brought our dead man home. Flew his body back, faxed the obits to the local papers, called the priests, the sexton, the florists and stonecutter. We act out things we cannot put into words.

Back in 1963, I can remember my father saying that the reason we had funerals and open caskets was so we might confront what he called 'the reality of death'. I think he'd heard that at one of these conferences. Jessica Mitford had just sold a million copies of *The American Way of Death* and Evelyn Waugh had already weighed in with *The Loved One* and talk had turned at cocktail parties to 'barbaric rituals' and 'morbid curiosities'. The mortuary associations were scrambling for some cover. Clergy and educators and psychologists—the new clergy—were assembled to say it served some purpose after all, was emotionally efficient, psychologically correct, to do what we'd been doing all along. The track record was pretty good on this. We'd been doing—the species, not the undertakers—more or less, the same thing for millennia: looking up while digging down, trying to make some sense of it all, disposing of our dead with efficient pause to say they'd lived in ways different from rocks and rhododendrons and even orang-utans and that those lives were worth mentioning and those lives were worth remembering.

Then John F. Kennedy was shot dead and Lee Harvey Oswald and we spent the end of November that year [1963] burying them—the first deaths in our lives that took for most of us boomers. All the other TV types got shot on *Gunsmoke* on a Friday and turned up on *Bonanza*, looking fit by Sunday night. But Kennedy was one of those realities of death my father must have been talking about and though we saw his casket and cortège and little John John saluting and the widow in her sunglasses, we never saw Kennedy dead, most of us, until years later when pictures of the autopsy were released and we all went off to the movies to see what really happened. In the interim, rumours circulated about Kennedy not being dead at all but hooked to some secret and expensive hardware, brainless but breathing. And when the Zapruder film convinced us that he must have died, still we lionised the man beyond belief. Of course, once we saw him dead in the pictures, his face, his body, he became human again: loveable and imperfect, memorable and dead.

RESPECT FOR THE DEAD AND RESPECT FOR LIFE

And as I watch my generation labour to give their teenagers and young adults some 'family values' between courses of pizza and Big Macs, I think maybe Gladstone had it right. I think my father did. They understood that the meaning of life is connected, inextricably, to the meaning of death; that mourning is a romance in reverse, and if you love, you grieve and there are no exceptions—only those who do it well and those who don't. And if death is regarded as an embarrassment or an inconvenience, if the dead are regarded as a nuisance from whom we seek a hurtled riddance, then life and the living are in for like treatment: McFunerals, McFamilies, McMarriage, McValues. This is the mathematical precision the old Britisher was talking about and what my father was talking about when he said we'd know what to do.

Thus tending to his death, his dead body, had for me the same importance as being present for the births of my sons, my daughter. Some expert on Oprah might call this 'healing'. Another on Donahue might say 'cathartic'. Over on Geraldo it might have 'scarred him for life'. And Sally Jesse Whatshername might mention 'making good choices'. As if they were talking about men who cut umbilical cords and change diapers or women who confront their self-esteem issues or their date-rapists.

A FUNERAL IS GRIEF THERAPY

It is not about choices or functions or psychological correctness. A dead body has had its options limited, its choices narrowed. It is an old thing in the teeth of which we do what has been done because it is the thing to do. We needn't reinvent the wheel or make the case for it, though my generation always seems determined to.

And they are at it over on the island. Trying to reinvent the funeral as 'a vehicle for the healthy expression of grief' which, of course, it is; or as 'a brief therapy for the acutely bereaved' which, of course, it is. There will be talk of 'stages', 'steps', 'recovery'. Someone will mention 'aftercare', 'post-funeral service follow-up', Widow to Widow programmes, Mourners Anonymous? And in the afternoons they'll play nine holes or go snorkeling or start cocktails too early and after dinner they'll go dancing then call home to check in with their offices just before they go to bed. Maybe I'll take the boat over tomorrow. Maybe some of the old timers are there—men of my father's generation, men you could call in the middle of the night if there was trouble. They remind me of my father and of Gladstone. Maybe they'll say I remind them of him.

PERIODICAL BIBLIOGRAPHY

The following articles have been selected to supplement the diverse views presented in this chapter. Addresses are provided for periodicals not indexed in the *Readers' Guide to Periodical Literature*, the *Alternative Press Index*, the *Social Sciences Index*, or the *Index to Legal Periodicals and Books*.

Dianne Bergant	"Death in the Family," *U.S. Catholic*, April 1996.
Harold Brodkey	"This Wild Darkness," *New Yorker*, February 5, 1996.
Karen Catchpole	"Oh My God, She's Dead!" *Mademoiselle*, July 1995.
Janet Choi	"Letting Go: All I'd Learned in Med School Wasn't Enough to Save My Uncle," *Mademoiselle*, April 1995.
Margaret M. Conway	"A Shattered Spirit: Grief and Self-Discovery," *America*, December 30, 1995.
Ginny Cunningham	"How to Pay Your Respects to Grief," *U.S. Catholic*, July 1994.
Mary Beth Danielson	"Broken Days: Opening Up Our Schedules to Life," *Utne Reader*, July/August 1994.
Richard T. Gill	"Whatever Happened to the American Way of Death?" *Public Interest*, Spring 1996.
Kathryn Harrison	"What Remains: The Lure of Relics in a Faithless Age," *Harper's Magazine*, December 1995.
James M. Kennedy	"Just Being There," *Reader's Digest*, February 1996.
David Loxterkamp	"'Don't Look Back': A Mother's Farewell," *Commonweal*, October 25, 1996.
Thomas Lynch	"Burying the Ungrateful Dead," *Harper's Magazine*, April 1995.
Alane Salierno Mason	"The Reconciliation of Unbelief," *Commonweal*, March 22, 1996.
Betsy Okonski	"Just Say Something," *Newsweek*, May 6, 1996.
William J. O'Malley	"Making Sense of Suffering and Death," *America*, April 13, 1996.
Anna Quindlen	"The Oft-Invisible Burden of Survivors," *U.S. Catholic*, July 1994.
Gerald Sittser	"The Life and Death We Don't Deserve," *Christian Century*, January 17, 1996.
Lois Greene Stone	"Living Humanism: Dealing with Death and Parents," *Humanist*, May/June 1996.

CHAPTER 4

IS DEATH THE END OF LIFE?

Chapter Preface

In 1975, Raymond A. Moody Jr. published *Life After Life*, his investigation of near-death experiences. As a doctor, Moody had the opportunity to interview a number of patients who had "died"—had suffered heart failure and stopped breathing—and been resuscitated. He discovered that many revived patients tell similar stories of their dying experience. In the typical near-death experience, as described by Moody, the patient floats above his body and looks down upon the room. Next, he travels through a tunnel toward a bright light. Upon reaching the light he encounters another person, a long-departed loved one or simply a being of light, who informs him that he must return to life. The publication of Moody's findings in *Life After Life* spawned a host of other near-death-experience accounts and a debate over their significance.

Moody's research convinced him that these patients' visions are proof of another existence following the death of the body. To support that conclusion, he points out that invariably near-death experiencers are spiritually transformed by the event, becoming happier, more at peace, and more fulfilled in life. Near-death patients return to life with "complete confidence that what we call death is just a passage into another level of reality," he states. The transformation that takes place in revived patients demonstrates the reality of the phenomenon as "a glimpse of the beyond," Moody asserts.

But others who have researched this phenomenon dispute Moody's conclusion. Susan Blackmore, a senior lecturer in psychology at the University of the West of England in Bristol, contends that the near-death experience is a physiological and psychological phenomenon rather than a supernatural one. The tunnel and light envisioned by the patients, she argues, are the effects of the neurochemical processes taking place in the brain as it dies. Other aspects of the experience, such as floating above the body and encountering a being, are interpretations of this physical process imposed by the patient as he or she tries to remember and make sense of the experience, in Blackmore's opinion. Though patients can be spiritually transformed by such a close encounter with death, Blackmore maintains, near-death experiences "provide no evidence for life after death."

While some researchers have been looking for ways to scientifically prove that life after death exists, other scientists have been searching for ways to extend life past the point of natural death. The viewpoints in the following chapter debate the possibility of cryonic preservation and of the existence of an afterlife.

"I . . . was given affirmation that yes, the Light is always there for all of us."

NEAR-DEATH EXPERIENCES ARE GLIMPSES OF THE AFTERLIFE

Kimberly Clark Sharp, interviewed by Guy Spiro

Kimberly Clark Sharp is the director of the Seattle chapter of the International Association for Near-Death Studies. She is also the author of *After the Light: What I Discovered on the Other Side of Life That Can Change Your World.* The following viewpoint is excerpted from an interview with Sharp by Guy Spiro, the publisher of the *Monthly Aspectarian: The World's New Age Magazine.* Sharp maintains that during her two near-death experiences she encountered God in the form of a being of light. From these events, she contends, she gained deep spiritual awareness and learned that death is not the end of life but a transition to a different form of existence. The purpose of the present life, she argues, is to prepare for the next one.

As you read, consider the following questions:

1. According to Sharp, what three aspects of earthly life do people take with them to the next life?
2. In the author's opinion, what is death?

From "A Conversation with Kimberly Clark Sharp" by Kimberly Clark Sharp, interviewed by Guy Spiro, the *Monthly Aspectarian: The World's New Age Magazine,* Online edition, November 1996 (www.lightworks.com). Reprinted by permission of the publisher.

The Monthly Aspectarian: *Kim, so many people have read your book,* After the Light, *about the beautiful, and the harrowing, aftereffects you've lived through since your near death experiences. What's important in your message at this point?*

Kimberly Clark Sharp: The bottom line is that the whole point of us being alive at this time can be summarized as a matter of faith. That faith would be that each of us has a purpose very specifically designed for us. That one does not weigh in more than another in God's eyes. Faith that we are never alone. We're surrounded at all times by invisibilities, some of whom help us, some of whom trip us up so that we know how it feels to fall—and some of whom help us to get back up again. And faith that our souls are eternal.

WHAT PEOPLE TAKE WITH THEM WHEN THEY DIE

When we die, we take three very important aspects of our lives on earth with us . . . and this goes on eternally; that is, we take our personalities. In my near death experience, the "I" that was "me" was not what was in my body but what was outside, observing. The scariest part for most people afraid of death is that afterward, we are not going to exist anymore as separate personalities. But indeed, we do. Along with our personalities, we take cognition along with us as well . . . and that involves memory. So—we take our memory with us, and that helps us in our life review, which in turn helps us understand what our purpose on earth has been—or, in the case of people who are going back, what the purpose will be hereafter. Thirdly, and most importantly, I might add, we take along the love that we've been given and that we have given to others who have been with us. It weighs in like currency. So my advice to people would be to be nice to everybody because that is our goal. That's our credit when our lives are over.

Isn't it funny how some of those old sayings that got rejected in the past decades, like "Virtue is its own reward," turn out to be true?

Yeah! I also want readers to know something about me, Guy. That I come from the midwest, although I've lived in Seattle since my near death experience. I'm from Johnson County, Kansas, outside of Kansas City, the third highest income per capita in the country. . . . I grew up with the proverbial "silver spoon" and had no intention of altering my lifestyle until after my near death experience. I was one of those people who not only was pronounced dead and down for an hour and a half, which is an extraordinarily, miraculously long period of time, but also I'm one of those people who did a one-eighty in changing from materialistic, selfish—well, let's put it this way: I thought service came in two forms, sterling and uniformed. I also want readers to know that since my near death experience, I've gotten my Master's in social work, I've become a clinical assistant professor at the University of Washington, I teach in the School of Medicine at the University of Washington. My work with dying people has received a lot of honors. For instance, in 1987 I was named one of the forty most influential people in the Pacific Northwest for my work with death and dying. And I'm currently running the world's oldest and largest group for near death experiencers, the Seattle International Association for Near-Death Studies. I want readers to know about my credibility but at the same time, I also want readers to know that I'm called the Erma Bombeck of the near death movement—and that was bestowed upon me by Erma Bombeck herself.

UNCONDITIONAL LOVE DURING THE NEAR-DEATH EXPERIENCE

Two NDErs [near-death experiencers] I interviewed made similar comments. One, who had an NDE from a heart attack, said that during his experience he encountered "a diaphanous Christ-like figure" with outstretched hands emanating a loving light. He then knew how well-loved he was due to this figure. He could feel the love, and he wanted to be enveloped by that love.

The other NDEr, "Joan," . . . said the bright white light for her was love that she brought back with her. It was a love that "circulated" through her entire being.

William J. Serdahely, *Journal of Near-Death Studies*, Fall 1996.

How did that come about?

After the Light is a funny book in the Erma Bombeck sense, and any speech I give literally leaves people in tears from laughter and poignancy. I'm not a very serious person when it comes to this subject, and I have a lot of funny stories to tell.

In February 1996 I was in Phoenix doing book signings and lectures and Erma heard a radio spot I did. She called the radio station and said, "By golly, you're the Erma Bombeck of the near death movement." Then called me in Seattle and asked me for a personally inscribed copy of the book. She loved it, and took it with her to California where she went for a liver transplant, and she died there. One of her representatives called and told me how much the book meant to her—and it would, because it's funny.

Near-Death Experiences of the Light

I know you've had two near death experiences.

I've had two experiences in the Light.

The first one was interesting to me because you didn't know you were having a near death experience. Most of the experiences you read about are people who know they've been blown out of their body. But you didn't even know you were having an NDE until you were being sent back and you realized something was wrong.

Yes; until that time, it felt more real, more normal and more sensible to be with God in the form of a magnificent Light than it was to be in my body. This was what was real. Everything else paled in comparison. It was like I was awakening from a dream and remembering where I had come from.

And in this first experience you didn't do a life review—and you didn't have the tunnel that others who've experienced NDEs have written about.

Right. I pretty much went straight to "the big G," and actually God—I call my Creator—I was with that which made me, and this Light that I was in was so loving . . . and it was personal love; it was directed absolutely at me. Also, communication between us was so easy, so much better than communication on earth although it wasn't English or any kind of spoken language; a combination of math and music is how we both communicated. I asked a lot of questions. The answers I got back were very simple . . . we don't have time for me to go into all the aspects of everything I learned—that's why I wrote a book. But it was fantastic because the answers were so simple that if I'd had a head, I would have smacked it—in the sense of "Gee, I should have had a V-8." It wasn't until I was sent back that I remembered there was another existence. But "death" did not occur to me because I basically don't understand death. Death, to me, even to this day, is not an end; it's a transition.

The Light Is Always There

In your second experience, you must have gone A-ha! I know what this is!

I did. I did. In my second experience—it was a spontaneous one eleven years later while I was driving my car. . . . I had just had a woo-woo, which is my scientific term for all the spiritual weirdness that happens. And that had just happened, a woo-woo. I was zipping along in my car when the dashboard faded, everything faded, and again I had cognition—and my joy at being reunited with this Light was . . . it's incomprehensible to others how happy I was. To my amazement, I found myself at a curb in my car, three hours later. My experience this time was more like a romance, it was so heartfelt. I again was given affirmation that yes, the Light is always there for all of us. It was incredible.

I came out of that experience in an accelerated form of spirituality that lasted for many years . . . and then eventually credit cards and car pools and paint peeling on the house—the projects of life—began to take over again and I realized how important it was to keep a *balance* between that which would enchant all of us, which would distract all of us from our life's work: the full-blown knowledge of how much is out there to help us through our life. Balancing that with child care and home care and job care and the mundaneness of our lives . . . which is just as important, because we need to function where we've been sent! And we've been sent here, to the land of checkbooks. My favorite saying is an old one: "Before enlightenment, chop wood, carry water. After enlightenment, chop wood, carry water." Truer words were never spoken. I encourage people on spiritual paths [to stay connected with their physical lives], to remember their zip codes.

Yeah, I agree. The world is a theme park and I'm on the Guy ride.

I'm on the roller coaster; I've had two experiences. However, I have had so many other experiences in "regular" life with angels, with demons, with a whole lot of dead people. I've crammed all of that into the book.

Spiritual Awareness and Healing

I have one leg in this reality, the chop wood reality. I have another leg in the full-blown spiritual awareness. I don't even know what to call it: realm, I guess, or realms. It makes for a very interesting life because I've achieved that balance, but it can be crazy-making at times. Five years ago, I was told I had eight to ten months to live, and it was through my faith that all would be well that I survived. Also the fact that I'm not afraid of death . . . and I had all that energy, the energy that I would have spent being terrified, left over to apply to my healing. The spiritual door to healing opened to me at that time. That seemed to be the lesson of that experience. There was that and lots of other lessons.

There are not many people who could look me in the eye and tell me their stories, to whom I could not say, "I know how you feel." The balance of the richness of my spiritual life has been in suffering. I've lost a baby. I've lost a fiancé. I lost my health. But also, I've been committed to the tender loving care of other people, particularly those who are dying and are utterly terrified. So I've paid my dues—let's put it that way. Now, I feel like I'm here simply to enjoy "the amusement park of life," to use your metaphor. Right now, my life is one of getting a lot of rewards. I mean, the book has been a pinch-me kind of experience.

It seems right that you should have a book, too.

Well, I wrote it to help people. The pinch-me part has been the awesomeness of the degree of that help. I mean, people who have called me who have been on the brink of suicide and who have gotten help instead because they were given hope by reading the book. People who were dying, who were afraid. Whose children are dying, and they had no hope.

| "To take the word of the [near-death experiencer] about the ultimate destiny of the soul is unwarranted."

NEAR-DEATH EXPERIENCES MAY NOT BE GLIMPSES OF THE AFTERLIFE

Douglas Groothuis

In the following viewpoint, Douglas Groothuis maintains that many accounts of near-death experiences (NDEs) conflict with the Christian vision of the afterlife. According to Groothuis, many near-death survivors describe encounters with a nonjudgmental being of light who affirms that humans can transcend their earthly existence—a scenario that conforms to New Age beliefs. But Christians believe that at death, God will punish the wicked and reward the righteous, he contends. Because many NDE stories contradict Christian teachings about death, he argues, these descriptions of the afterlife should be distrusted. Groothuis, a professor of philosophy and religion at Denver Seminary, is the author of *Deceived by the Light* and *The Soul in Cyberspace*.

As you read, consider the following questions:

1. According to Groothuis, what did Betty Eadie conclude based on her near-death experience?
2. How does researcher Maurice Rawlings define the "religion of the resuscitated," according to the author?
3. What are some ways in which accounts of near-death experiences conflict with each other, according to the author?

From "To Heaven and Back?" by Douglas Groothuis, *Christianity Today*, April 3, 1995. Reprinted by permission of the author.

In early 1993 I received a call from an embarrassed radio announcer at a Christian radio station in Washington. He confessed that he had recently interviewed a local woman who he now thought may have been a "wolf in sheep's clothing." Her name was Betty Eadie, and she was the author of an allegedly Christian book, Embraced by the Light. In it she gives an elaborate account of her near-death experience (NDE). The dedication reads: "To the Light, my Lord and Savior Jesus Christ, to whom I owe all that I have. He is the 'staff' that I lean on; without him I would fall."

I consented to do a follow-up telephone interview on the subject of near-death experiences and so purchased and read Eadie's book.

A VIEW OF THE AFTERLIFE?

As I read the short but fantastic account of Eadie's experience on "the other side," I quickly discerned that the "Jesus Christ" to whom Eadie dedicated her book was not the same one the New Testament attests. Eadie's Jesus, an amorphously benevolent being of light, surrounded her in such a way that she could not tell where her "light" stopped and his began. Eadie concluded, based on her NDE, that Jesus was a being completely separate from the Father, that he would do nothing to offend her (so she should stop regretting past deeds), that humans are not sinful creatures by nature, that human "spirit beings" assisted the "Heavenly Father" at the Creation, and that, despite appearances, the world is bereft of tragedy. She concluded, "I knew that I was worthy to be with him, to embrace him."

On a recent 20/20 television program, Eadie elaborated on her theology. She told Hugh Downs that her NDE informed her that those who had died in the Holocaust had chosen their fates before birth. This revelation was supposed to ease the anguish of the problem of evil. Yet one would have to question the intelligence of these preincarnate Jewish spirits in willfully choosing this ghastly demise. By attempting to eliminate tragedy, she impugns the victims and exonerates the perpetrators, none of who will suffer in hell.

As I discussed and challenged these claims during the radio interview, several callers objected. How could I criticize this "nice lady"? One caller insisted that Eadie had experienced something of God but had simply confused some of the details. He told me "not to throw out the baby with the bath water."

But there is no baby here. As I told the caller, "What Mrs. Eadie has right is that there is a God, and there is an afterlife."

And one doesn't need to die to reach these conclusions.

My radio interview took place before Eadie's book began its meteoric rise to the top of the *New York Times* bestseller list (where it stayed for over a year and a half) and before she became an instant celebrity, appearing on the *Oprah Winfrey Show* and 20/20. Why would purported Christians want to believe Eadie's unbiblical account of the afterlife? And why are Christian bookstores frequently pestered to stock her book?

Although a large majority of Americans believe in God or some Higher Power, their religious beliefs are often self-styled, ill-conceived, and sloppily syncretistic. Because of secularization and religious pluralism, religious beliefs tend to be restricted to the private, subjective realm where they are isolated from public scrutiny. As a result, a plethora of religious expressions clamor for acceptance, many of which are falsely assumed to be "Christian." Few Americans need to be convinced that there is an afterlife (although, not surprisingly, more believe in heaven than in hell), but now a whole raft of near-death experiencers (NDEers) are eager to supply the metaphysical details. These accounts often conflict with each other and usually contradict biblical revelation.

THE BIRTH OF A TREND

Twenty years ago, most Americans believed in the afterlife, but most assumed that it applied to the dead only. Raymond Moody's little best-selling book *Life After Life* changed all that. Moody reported the experiences of 50 survivors of "clinical death" who claimed to have experienced another world. The individual experiences varied, but Moody identified several recurring features: leaving the body, observing the events surrounding one's "death," a rapid trip through a tunnel to a "Being" of Light, a review of one's life, the appearance of deceased relatives and/or angels, and the return to the body.

Moody also reported that while none experienced anything akin to the biblical picture of heaven or hell, almost all returned to physical life with new vigor and little or no fear of death.

Psychologist Kenneth Ring supplemented Moody's work with the rigorous *Life at Death*, which was followed by cardiologist Michael Sabom's *Recollections of Death*. Although differing from Moody's findings at certain points, Ring and Sabom corroborated the overall pattern of the NDE and helped put it squarely on the scientific map. Both acknowledged the explanations for the NDE that reduced it to merely a psychological, pharmacological, or physiological phenomenon devoid of anything spiritual. However, their investigations concluded that at least some

NDEs involved actual out-of-body experiences beyond the realm of clinical death.

More recently, Melvin Morse, a pediatrician in Seattle, has captured national attention with his research into children's experiences with NDEs. Morse's *Closer to the Light* concludes that NDEs must be taken seriously and not dismissed as delusional because of the children's consistent testimony, their innocence, and the fact that their experiences could not be explained on the basis of medication.

Because of work by people like Moody, Ring, Sabom, and Morse, the NDE is now a readily available category of paranormal experience. The International Association for Near-Death Studies, founded in 1981, helps NDEers understand their experience while educating others, and it also publishes a quarterly newsletter and an interdisciplinary academic journal.

First-person NDE accounts like *Embraced by the Light* and, more recently, *Saved by the Light*, by Dannion Brinkley, are selling briskly, the latter perhaps eclipsing Eadie in sensational appeal with his account of receiving mysterious counsel from 13 luminous beings.

NDEs are increasingly being taken as visionary and even prophetic, notwithstanding their unbiblical and illogical themes. Eadie's book, despite (or maybe because of) its artless matter-of-fact manner of describing cosmic visions, refuses to die. The paperback and the audio versions of *Embraced by the Light* have already been released.

Why this popularity?

THE RELIGION OF THE RESUSCITATED

In addition to the desire of creatures stranded "east of Eden" to discover what—if anything—lies beyond death's door, the interest in NDE accounts can be explained by another American religious tendency: immediate individual spirituality.

Eadie makes no mention of the fact that she is a Mormon, either in the book or on her tours. Brinkley lays claim to no institutional church connections and makes no pretense at being a saintly fellow. Yet both claim to have met ultimate reality face-to-face without the assistance of any religious institution, human mediation, or historical connection. They were There; now they Know; and we should listen, especially since the news they bring is so consoling.

These claims of blissful unmediated divine experience on "the other side" are producing what Christian NDE researcher Maurice Rawlings calls "the religion of the resuscitated." In his book *To Hell and Back*, he describes this ersatz religion as embracing the belief in an enjoyable life after death with no fear of divine judgment. It dispenses with traditional dogmas of sin and the need for salvation, asserting instead that one must simply grow in knowledge and love, both vaguely defined. One NDEer in Moody's studies who had previously been a loyal Lutheran claimed that "the Lord isn't interested in doctrine." Hence, a kind of simplistic syncretism and universalism is affirmed.

As John Weldon and John Ankerberg point out in *The Facts on Life After Death*, this claim asserts that, on the one hand, we are exhorted to grow in knowledge while, on the other hand, we are barred from specific doctrinal affirmations about God, such as there being a narrow road that leads to life and a broad road leading to destruction (Matt. 7:13).

The "religion of the resuscitated" also usually affirms the unlimited potential of humans. Eadie speaks of Jesus as her "Savior," but it is difficult to see how he functions as such given the role she claims for herself. She helped in the creation of the world as a preincarnate spirit; she briefly experienced omniscience (conveniently lost upon her returning); her thoughts have "tremendous power" to create reality; her soul and that of others progress eternally (a Mormon doctrine); and, as mentioned, she is worthy of Jesus' embrace. There is little room for "amazing grace" here.

Other NDEers make similar claims about unlimited capacities triggered through the experience. In *Life at Death*, Kenneth Ring avers that the NDE connects one with a "higher self," the pantheistic God within.

The "religion of the resuscitated" perpetuates the utopian hope that the prevalence of NDEs may be sparking a new evolutionary development in human consciousness. In this and other respects, the NDE phenomenon conforms to recurring New Age aspirations and predilections. Once freed from the fear of death and awakened to their latent power, humans may transcend their self-imposed crises and enter the New Age.

NEAR-DEATH EXPERIENCES AND THE CHRISTIAN AFTERLIFE

How might discerning Christians sort out this material theologically and apologetically?

Some skeptics have dismissed the NDE as simply the hallucinations of a dying brain, manufacturing a bogus sense of transcendence in the face of destruction. Susan Blackmore's *Dying to Live* rigorously attempts to explain (and explain away) the NDE on the basis of physiological factors alone. Despite her ardor, Blackmore's theories fail to capture every aspect of NDEs. A legitimate supernatural element does seem to exist with some NDEs, especially concerning reports of people accurately describing physical events that occurred after they have left their bodies at the point of clinical death.

NEAR-DEATH EXPERIENCES AND NEW AGE BELIEFS

New Agers continually stress how wonderful the near-death experience is—one allegedly feels inexplicable love, joy, and peace. Such sensations, they say, are a key element of an NDE. That some people have experienced these feelings is not in question, but that they alone describe NDEs is disputed by other research that indicates that some people have had hellish experiences during their NDEs. For instance, Carol Zaleski, a professor of religion at Smith College [in Northampton, Massachusetts], records not only the heavenly but the hellish descriptions of NDEs in her historical treatment of this phenomenon. Her book *Otherworld Journeys: Accounts of Near-Death Experiences in Medieval and Modern Times* is at the same time widely respected for its academic excellence *and* is troubling to some New Agers who have assumed that NDEs confirm their belief in a nonjudgmental God and a punishment-free afterlife for all people.

Yet even if some NDEs produce spiritual experiences, that does not resolve the problem of conflicting testimonies. Some people come back believing in reincarnation, some don't; some near-death experiencers do not claim to experience God but only a light; some speak of bliss; some speak of a hellish NDE during which they experienced a sense of darkness and torment and the presence of evil beings intent upon drawing them into doom.

A Christian world-view can account for the negative NDEs as more than inexplicable aberrations or subjective projections. God may give a sinner a shocking taste of hell in order to awaken a healthy fear of God. . . .

But what do we make of the blissful NDEs, such as that of Betty Eadie, that contradict a biblical view of the afterlife?

Although the evidence suggests that people sometimes experience some sort of spiritual reality apart from the body during their clinical deaths, this does not guarantee that all who claim NDEs have actually had one, that what people experience reflects ultimate reality, or that their testimonies are true. Despite her claims, there is no hard evidence that Betty Eadie actually died.

She waited nearly 20 years before publishing her material, refuses to release her medical records, and claims that the physician in charge of her medical crisis has since died. The account of her death in her book lacks the ring of truth.

NEAR-DEATH ENCOUNTERS WITH EVIL?

In addition, although some NDEs may be real experiences beyond the body, we should ask, "How reliable are these experiences?" Given what Jesus taught about demonic deception, it makes sense that the Evil One would delight in convincing souls that they need not fear the judgment of a holy God.

An NDE reported by Ring in *Heading Toward Omega* involved a being who consoled a fretting woman that "there are no sins." Many other NDEs agree. Yet if Jesus' words are true, we are, in fact, enslaved to sin and will die in our sins if we do not believe in the Son of Man who came to seek and to save the lost. As Blaise Pascal astutely warned in *Pensées*, "Between heaven and hell is only this life, which is the most fragile thing in the world."

Rawlings and others have given accounts of NDEs that seem to involve an encounter with the God of the Bible because their experiences concur with what we know about God's holiness and love. Bernard J. Klamecki, a medical doctor, reports in *The Crisis of Homosexuality* that a young man told him that he clinically died after a massive dose of antibiotics to treat a venereal disease. The man left his body and encountered "the Omnipotent One," who lovingly told him that he had not used his gifts to glorify Christ. After the man's resuscitation, he abandoned his homosexual way of life, became a Christian, and joined a supportive Christian community. The combination of Christ's love and moral instruction in this NDE makes sense theologically.

NEAR-DEATH EXPERIENCES ARE NOT EXPERIENCES OF DEATH

However, NDEs by themselves cannot establish a reliable theology. Gary Habermas and J.P. Moreland rightly argue in *Immortality* that the NDE phenomenon helps establish that the soul can exist apart from the body for a short time, but that this is a "minimalist" claim because it says nothing of the final state of the soul. Those returning from near-death may have clinically died (indicated by a lack of heartbeat and/or brain waves), but they have not experienced biological or irreversible death. Nor have any been resurrected. Therefore, to take the word of the NDEer about the ultimate destiny of the soul is unwarranted, given the penultimate state of the NDE itself.

A genuine NDE cannot be compared to the final eschatological state wherein "every knee shall bow and every tongue confess that Jesus Christ is Lord" (Phil. 2:10–11). The disembodied soul is still subject to the deception wrought by the "ruler of the kingdom of the air" (Eph. 2:2) and his minions, who are not above appearing as angels of light (2 Cor. 11:14). One may encounter a deceptive light that lacks truth.

Considering the conflicting testimonies of near-death experiences, their frequent disagreement with biblical revelation, the possibility of demonic deception, and their penultimate nature, we should dismiss the "religion of the resuscitated" and instead embrace the eternal certainties offered by the One who experienced death, burial, resurrection, and ascension to the place of unmatched authority. He alone has the last word on matters of life and death.

| "[Near-death experiences] provide no evidence for life after death."

NEAR-DEATH EXPERIENCES ARE NOT GLIMPSES OF AN AFTERLIFE

Hayden Ebbern, ɔean Mulligan, and Barry L. Beyerstein

It has long been known that the brain continues to work for a few minutes after the heart and lungs have stopped, argue Hayden Ebbern, Sean Mulligan, and Barry L. Beyerstein in the following viewpoint. They contend that near-death experiences (NDEs) provide insight into the brain's functioning during this interval. These experiences, they maintain, are simply hallucinations and do not prove that life after death exists. At the time that this viewpoint was written, Ebbern was an undergraduate in psychology and Mulligan was a graduate student in biological sciences at Simon Fraser University, Burnaby, British Columbia, Canada. Beyerstein is a professor of psychology and a researcher at the Brain Behavior Laboratory at Simon Fraser University.

As you read, consider the following questions:

1. In the view of psychologists and neuroscientists, cited by the authors, how does the brain construct a model of reality?
2. In the opinion of the authors, what is the agenda of the field of near-death studies?
3. In what other types of hallucinations do the elements of the typical NDE occur, according to the authors?

From "Maria's Near-Death Experience: Waiting for the Other Shoe to Drop" by Hayden Ebbern, Sean Mulligan, and Barry L. Beyerstein, *Skeptical Inquirer*, July/August 1996; © CSICOP. Reprinted by permission.

Skeptics enter most debates at a disadvantage because they are usually forced to cast doubt on comforting beliefs. The idea that so-called near-death experiences, NDEs for short, could count as evidence for survival of the soul after death is perhaps the most comforting belief of all. Since physician Raymond Moody coined the term "near-death experience" to describe a reasonably consistent set of experiences recalled by about a third of those who are resuscitated after near-fatal incidents, such descriptions have been welcomed with enthusiasm by a large segment of the public.

Susan Blackmore has described near-death experience as follows: "For many experiencers, their adventures seem unquestionably to provide evidence for life after death, and the profound effects the experience can have on them is just added confirmation. By contrast, for many scientists these experiences are just hallucinations produced by the dying brain and of no more interest than an especially vivid dream. So which is right? . . . neither is quite right: NDEs provide no evidence for life after death, and we can best understand them by looking at neurochemistry, physiology, and psychology; but they are much more interesting than any dream. . . . Any satisfactory theory . . . leads us to questions about minds, selves, and the nature of consciousness."

DEFINING CONSCIOUSNESS AND SOUL

Historically, philosophers have used the term mind to refer to the subjective awareness of one's self and its surroundings and the experience of imagining, planning, and willing our actions. Psychologists and neuroscientists generally prefer the term consciousness when referring to this inner stream of perceptions, images, memories, and feelings. It is from them that the brain assembles the conscious model it experiences as reality. By mixing inference with sensory inputs, body images, emotions, and stored memories, the brain constructs our sense of an ongoing self dwelling in a physical body, surrounded by a real world of objects and events. In religious lore, the terms soul or spirit encompass not only this subjective awareness of the self and its whereabouts, but also the belief that this mental tableau is a manifestation of a divine essence each individual is thought to possess. Believers consider souls nonmaterial, usually immortal. In what follows, mind and consciousness will refer to secular, naturalistic depictions of mental awareness. Soul or spirit will be reserved for when the holder's views imply that this awareness of the self is somehow supernatural, separable from the body, and capable of surviving death (i.e., in an "afterlife"). NDEs are only one example of episodes in which the brain's construction of reality breaks down temporarily and allows the self model to feel as if it were pure spiritual essence, no longer attached to a physical body.

The NDE typically begins with a sense of serenity and relief, followed by a feeling that the self is leaving the body (the "out-of-body experience," or OBE). From this vantage point, the supposedly disembodied spirit sometimes feels that it is observing attempts to revive its lifeless body. A subset of those who reach the OBE stage further report being propelled through a spiral tunnel toward a bright light. For some, the light eventually resolves into a significant religious figure, deceased relative or friend, or vista of paradise. As rescue procedures begin to take effect, these patients often report feeling great reluctance at being pulled back into the painful, uncertain, everyday world.

THE SEARCH FOR PROOF OF AN AFTERLIFE

Virtually every book retelling this now-familiar story achieves best-seller status and reaps substantial rewards for its author.

James Alcock provided several insights into the motivations underlying this fervent longing for "proof" of an afterlife. He also suggested an explanation for why the will to believe so readily overcomes the desire to examine the evidence critically:

> Intellectually capable of foreseeing that they will one day die, yet emotionally too frail to accept that physical death may indeed be the end of their existence, human beings have long clung to the idea that life continues beyond the grave.

Alcock reminds us that survival beyond death lies at the core of almost all formal religions and that protecting this hope was also a major impetus for the founding of the modern discipline of parapsychology. Alcock was referring in the latter statement to the eminent group of British scholars and statesmen who in the nineteenth century banded together to form the Society for Psychical Research. Disturbed by the implications of modern science for their Christian worldview, these members of the intelligentsia espoused the goal of establishing scientific proof for the existence of an immortal soul.

Reports of NDEs appeared earlier than the nineteenth century, however. One of the earliest accounts is that of a soldier's supposed return from death, found in Plato's *Republic*. The Bible too is replete with stories of people raised from the dead, as are the sacred texts of most other faiths. Although reports of NDEs have shown up over the centuries, the appearance rate seems to have increased dramatically in recent times. This is likely due to vast improvements in emergency medicine, coupled with a world-wide resurgence of religious fundamentalism (a twentieth-century movement among Christians, Jews, and Muslims that advocates the literal interpretation of their respective sacred writings). The spiritual interpretation of NDEs is reinforced by the mass media, which prosper by pandering to public longings of all sorts, including the desire for life after death.

BRAIN ACTIVITY DURING A NEAR-DEATH EXPERIENCE

The [near-death] experience [of passing through a tunnel] is not a brain in trauma as has been suggested; it is the experience of a brain passing away. . . . The mere passage of the brain seems to take place in layers as the outer neurotransmitters fail to fire and create the tunnel effect. When the tunnel closes, we are dead. Now, for those of us lucky enough to come back, a reversed tunnel effect takes place as the neurotransmitters begin to fire again. The light, of course, is the brightness of any room seen by the eyes, through closed eyelids, that had ceased to register any light at all. A bit unnerving, yes, but spooky, no.

Laura Darlene Lansberry, *Skeptical Inquirer*, Summer 1994.

The concept of immortality is, in the final analysis, a metaphysical proposition that can only be accepted or rejected on faith. While faith alone used to be sufficient to bolster such convictions, the growing prestige of science has left many sophisticated believers uneasy in the absence of more solid proof of an afterlife. In response, a field known as "near-death studies" has emerged with the thinly veiled agenda of providing a scientific gloss for religious views of an afterlife. About the same time, another field emerged known as "anomalistic psychology." It accepts that experiences such as NDEs and OBEs can seem compellingly real to those who have them, but offers many reasons to doubt their reality outside the mind of the percipient. Anomalistic psychology seeks naturalistic explanations for various seemingly supernatural states of consciousness based on sound psychological and neurophysiological research.

DUALISM: SEPARATION OF MIND AND BODY

To accept notions such as survival after death, disembodied spirits, and a host of other parapsychological phenomena, one must also adopt some form of the philosophical doctrine known as "dualism." Dualism asserts that the mind is fundamentally different from the physical body, and this is essentially equivalent to the religious concept of an "immaterial soul." If dualism is correct, it is possible, some say, for mind or consciousness to disengage temporarily from the body but still retain self-awareness and the ability to gather information and interact physically with the environment. Many dualists also believe that their spiritual selves are immortal and that these spiritual selves will eventually abandon their physical bodies and assume a separate existence in some other realm. All of this is impossible from the standpoint of "material monists" who assert that the mind is equivalent to and inseparable from brain function.

Not surprisingly, NDE accounts are welcomed by many occultists because they appear to be a major impediment to the materialist worldview they find so distasteful. Likewise, in fundamentalist circles, NDEs are hailed as a vindication for various spiritual teachings.

Materialists readily concede that the subjective experiences of the NDE feel very real. Indeed, they contend that NDEs helped suggest the concept of an immortal soul to our ancestors in the first place. Despite the subjective realness of the NDE, however, modern neuroscience offers not only a wealth of reasons to doubt the possibility of disembodied minds, but it also provides much evidence that the compelling subjective phenomena of the NDE can be generated by known brain mechanisms. Believers counter that the NDE seems too real to have been a dream or hallucination, but they forget that what we mean by the term hallucination is an internally generated experience so detailed, emotional, and believable that it is indistinguishable from ordinary perceptions of reality.

Brain Functioning During Cardiopulmonary Arrest

It is also important to note that NDEs are always reported by people who presume they have died, but have not really died. Cardiopulmonary arrest (C.P.A.)—i.e., stoppage of the heart and lungs—was once an adequate definition of death. With the advent of modern resuscitation techniques, however, it became possible in some cases to restore breathing and pulse, often as long as several minutes after they had ceased. During C.P.A., the brain undergoes several biochemical and physiological changes, but by relying on its limited backup of stored oxygen and metabolic fuels, certain aspects of consciousness can be sustained, albeit in a somewhat degraded fashion. Thus, it is not surprising that there might be some residual memories from the time that one was dying, but not yet clinically dead.

That this minority of revived C.P.A. patients recall anything from the interval tells us more about how the brain creates our sense of self and the feeling that there is an external reality than it does about the possibility of an afterlife. Much can be learned from studying the orderly fashion in which these internally constructed models shut down when the brain is traumatized, but because those who have been revived did not reach the irreversible state of brain death, any experiences they recall cannot be said to have come from "the other side."

The subjective contents of the NDE are anything but unique to the onset of death. The basic elements of the NDE are common to hallucinations of various sorts. They are also found in psychedelic drug states, psychoses, and migraine and epileptic "auras." Similar experiences have even been reported in a surprisingly high proportion of those who panic during natural disasters, when they are psychologically traumatized but in no real physical danger.

If the components of the NDE have plausible roots in brain physiology, this undermines the argument that they are a glimpse of the afterlife rather than a rich and believable hallucination.

"If sufficient biological structure in dying patients can be preserved at low temperatures today, then recovery and healing by future medical technology is (in principle) possible."

CRYONIC SUSPENSION CAN EXTEND LIFE BEYOND DEATH

Alcor Life Extension Foundation

Cryonic freezing can preserve dying or recently deceased patients for possible future recovery, contends the Alcor Life Extension Foundation in the following viewpoint. Since low temperature freezing does not appear to significantly damage the brain cells where memory and personality are stored, Alcor argues, it is theoretically possible that medical techniques perfected in the future will be able to restore cryonically frozen individuals to life and health. Alcor publishes *Cryonics: Reaching for Tomorrow*, from which this viewpoint is excerpted.

As you read, consider the following questions:

1. In the authors' opinion, what is the necessary requirement for the success of cryonic preservation?
2. What types of tissues have been recovered from ultra-low temperatures, according to Alcor?
3. According to the authors, what is the extent of freezing injury in brain tissue related to?

From "The Case for Cryonics," in *Cryonics: Reaching for Tomorrow*, by the Alcor Life Extension Foundation, Online edition,1997 (www.alcor.org). Reprinted with permission.

The central idea of cryonics is simple: if sufficient biological structure in dying patients can be preserved at low temperatures today, then recovery and healing by future medical technology is (in principle) possible. This proposition is based on diverse but solid evidence from the fields of neurobiology, low temperature biology, and theoretical engineering.

Fact: Persistence of long-term memory and personality (all the basic elements which define us as individuals) does not require continuous brain function. Clinical experience demonstrates that memory and personality may be retained in persons who have had prolonged breaks in brain electrical activity (such as is caused by profound cooling). Recovery still follows, as long as injuries which prevent resumption of normal metabolism can be prevented or reversed.

Fact: Ultra-low temperatures can preserve fine brain structures indefinitely, including those such as the synapses and neuropil, which are currently thought to encode memory and personality.

Fact: Design outlines already exist for cell repair technologies which could be used to recover patients retaining such brain structures, even if they are imperfectly preserved. Moreover, the development of these technologies appears inevitable, given the continuing advances in methods for engineering at the molecular level.

Most of these facts are common knowledge within their respective disciplines, but their significance is not widely appreciated due to a failure to integrate them. Joint consideration of these facts compels the following conclusion: Low temperature preservation of the human body by means available today appears in principle to be reversible by future medicine—and therefore should be adequate to maintain patients during the interim.

THE CASE FOR PRESERVATION

A necessary requirement for the success of cryonics is that the brain be preserved with reasonable integrity. Are present freezing methods sufficient to accomplish this?

Contrary to popular belief, the freezing of living tissue is not a process of great destruction. Cells do not "burst" when they are frozen at moderate or slow rates of cooling (as when patients are placed into cryonic suspension). Slow cooling causes water to leave cells so that cell interiors seldom freeze at all. Instead, ice forms between cells, causing injury to cell membranes, enzymes, and other cell proteins by removing water from them. The extent of this injury can be greatly reduced by the use of cryoprotectants ("antifreeze" compounds such as glycerol), which reduce or completely prevent ice formation.

The limited nature of freezing injury at the cellular level is well illustrated by the great variety of tissues that can be recovered from ultra-low temperatures with present preservation technology. These include heart valves, corneas, skin, and even human embryos.

BRAIN PRESERVATION

At the time of this writing, no whole organ, including the brain, has ever been shown to recover normal function following warming from the temperatures required for long-term storage. Nevertheless, abundant evidence exists suggesting that high-quality brain preservation can be—and is being—achieved with current technology.

There is good evidence that whole brains can be easily recovered from high sub-zero temperatures.

Golden hamsters cooled until 60% of their brain water was converted into ice have demonstrated complete recovery with no behavioral abnormalities.

Isolated cat brains treated with 15% glycerol and cooled to −20 degrees C for five days have demonstrated return of normal brain function (as determined by EEG measurements) upon warming and perfusion with fresh donor blood. (It is notable that 15% glycerol would also result in freezing of approximately 60% of the brain liquid volume at this temperature.)

THE GOAL OF CRYONICS

The application of low temperature preservation technology to terminal patients today is called cryonic suspension. The goal of cryonic suspension and the technology of cryonics is the transport of today's terminal patients to a time in the future when cell repair technology is available, and restoration to full function and health is possible—a time when freezing damage is a fully reversible injury and cures exist for virtually all of today's diseases, including aging.

Alcor Life Extension Foundation, Cryonics: Reaching for Tomorrow, 1997.

Low sub-zero temperatures (below −130 degrees C) are required for long-term preservation of tissue. Unfortunately, the functional viability of whole brains cooled to these temperatures with proper cryoprotection has never been studied. We must therefore rely upon indirect evidence to evaluate the integrity of brains cooled to ultra-low temperatures. Listed below are some of the most significant facts to consider.

Rabbit brains warmed from −79 degrees C with 23% glycerol cryoprotection appear indistinguishable from unfrozen brains under light microscopy. (It should be noted that this result would not be expected to significantly differ even at much lower temperatures, since cooling below −79 degrees C does not cause additional injury.)

Individual brain cells typically exhibit very high survival rates following exposure to low sub-zero temperatures, even with only modest cryoprotection.

Electron microscopy shows that synapses (brain cell structures believed to be the sites of memory storage) retain their structure when cooled to low sub-zero temperatures without any cryoprotection.

These facts strongly suggest that good quality preservation of brain tissue occurs even at ultra-low temperatures.

RECOVERY FROM CRYONIC SUSPENSION IS POSSIBLE

Recovery of whole mammalian brains from high sub-zero temperatures and recovery of individual brain cells from low sub-zero temperatures show that brain tissue can spontaneously recover from significant amounts of freezing injury. How much injury can be expected in human cryonic suspension?

The extent of freezing injury in tissue is related to the percentage of water which freezes, which in turn is related to the cryoprotectant concentration. Human cryonic suspension procedures involve replacement of 30% or more of tissue water with cryoprotectant—a degree of protection which can be shown to limit freezing to less than 60% of tissue water at any sub-zero temperature.

Since whole brains are known to readily resume function following 60% freezing, cryonic suspension would seem to preserve the brain in very good condition. Even in the absence of any immediate ability to recover function, it is clear that the vast majority of biological structure is preserved.

| "Cryonics doesn't work and never
can."

CRYONIC SUSPENSION CANNOT EXTEND LIFE BEYOND DEATH

Phil Bagnall

In the following viewpoint, Phil Bagnall argues that although the thought of returning to life in the future is appealing, it is impossible to revive a person who has undergone the cryonic suspension process. Low temperature cryonic freezing of brains and other organs irreversibly damages the tissues, he maintains. Bagnall is a science writer in Wallsend, Northumbria, England.

As you read, consider the following questions:

1. According to Bagnall, what damage does freezing cause to cells?
2. In the author's view, what would be the advantages of returning to life in the future?
3. What happens to major organs when they are rapidly frozen to extremely low temperatures, according to the author?

From "Cold Comfort for Christmas" by Phil Bagnall, New Scientist, December 23-30, 1995; © New Scientist. Reprinted with permission.

W hat to buy my nearest and dearest this Christmas? I spent weeks worrying about it until someone suggested the gift of cryonic preservation. Not just yet, you understand, but after she's passed on. In the meantime, I could start a fund to help pay for the gift.

It did seem like a good idea. After all, we have spent a blissful 15 years together, so why shouldn't she find love in the 23rd century? It was only after I did a little research that I began to have some nagging doubts.

Cryonics, in case you're wondering, is the science of freezing someone in the hope that they can be revived at a later date. In the US it can cost between $40,000 and $140,000 and so is considerably more expensive than a conventional funeral in Britain. So only about 1000 people worldwide have expressed a serious desire to be cryonically preserved.

PROBLEMS WITH FREEZING CELLS

Even so, if you decide freezing is for you you will probably be in good company—though I'd better not mention anyone by name. And the people offering a cryonic service won't say who they have on their books, or should I say in their flasks. Freezing a body is far from easy. Ice crystals form inside the body's cells and become quite large and jagged, often puncturing delicate membranes causing cells to collapse. Salts build up and the acid-alkaline ratio changes, throwing the whole biological system into chaos.

To overcome this problem, the cryonics companies rapidly freeze bodies in vats of liquid nitrogen to below −196 °C. At this temperature most people believe all biochemical activity, including decay, ceases and the body can be preserved indefinitely. They also argue that rapid freezing—several degrees per second—prevents the build-up of large ice crystals and keeps cells intact for later resurrection.

The cryonics companies do not guarantee you a resurrection, only that you have a better chance than everyone else of being "re-born" at some time in the future. And just to ensure that you don't have a rude awakening you can specify the conditions under which you wish to return. So if, for example, you have suffered from chronic asthma, then you may wish to remain suspended until your problem can be cured.

I was quite taken with this idea. Waking up a few centuries from now would be a real eye opener. You could find out how the human race dealt with global warming, ozone depletion, overpopulation and dwindling rain forests. You would be able to see how many of the new discoveries made during your last years were developed into practical applications. And, of course, you'd be able to discover whether or not your National Lottery numbers ever came up.

Problems with Cryonic Suspension

How good an idea is [cryonics]? Conventional cryobiologists, the people who freeze sperm or the odd body part, are skeptical. They point to the extensive cell damage associated both with death and the degree of cooling required for a whole body or even a head. As . . . Arthur Rowe of NYU's School of Medicine, has explained, "believing cryonics could reanimate somebody who has been frozen is like believing you can turn hamburger back into a cow." In addition, even if enough cells can be revived, it is also far from clear, to say the least, that the patient's mind would have been preserved.

Andrew Stuttaford, *National Review*, September 2, 1996.

The only snag is that cryonics doesn't work and never can. Of the people who have thus far actually been frozen, about a third have been allowed to thaw out and been given more conventional funerals, mainly because the undertakers who promised to hold them in suspension for centuries went bankrupt after just a few years. A bit rough when you have had to find £90,000 [$140,000] in the hope of eternal life. But the real problem is with the state of the defrosted bodies.

What Happens to Frozen Bodies

When a human body is rapidly frozen to −196 °C and then held at that temperature, it undergoes a sort of thermal shock. Most of the major organs, including the heart, lungs, liver and kidneys, develop fissures and, quite literally, fall apart. In some cases major organs have been reduced to little more than dust, which is not much good if you needed them again in the dim and distant future when Britain gets a decent science budget and scientists work out how to bring you back to life.

"Ah, but we've got that problem cracked," the cryonics companies claim, though perhaps not in exactly those words. "We'll offer you the opportunity of neurosuspension." Their solution is to get rid of your body altogether and freeze just your head. It may sound gruesome but apparently you stand a better chance of resurrection if only your head is "preserved".

Call me an old sceptic, but I don't believe a word of it. To my way of thinking, the brain would fall apart. It doesn't matter whether you are talking about whole-body suspension or the cheaper $26,000 neurosuspension, no organs presently survive cryonic processing undamaged.

Which leaves me with my original problem of what to buy her for Christmas. Perhaps there's something in that idea of the Orbit of Rest in deep outer space.

PERIODICAL BIBLIOGRAPHY

The following articles have been selected to supplement the diverse views presented in this chapter. Addresses are provided for periodicals not indexed in the *Readers' Guide to Periodical Literature*, the *Alternative Press Index*, the *Social Sciences Index*, or the *Index to Legal Periodicals and Books*.

Richard Abanes	"Readers Embrace the Light," *Christianity Today*, March 7, 1994.
Betty J. Eadie	"Looking at Life," *Ladies' Home Journal*, January 1995.
John Garvey	"Christianity Isn't 'Spiritual': What 'Resurrection' Means," *Commonweal*, May 5, 1995.
Art Hilgart	"The West End Blues," *Humanist*, July/August 1996.
Wendy Kaminer	"The Latest Fashion in Irrationality: When the Inner Child Finds a Guardian Angel, Publishers Are in Heaven," *Atlantic Monthly*, July 1996.
John F. Kavanaugh	"After Life," *America*, April 29, 1995.
Laura Darlene Lansberry	"First-Person Report: A Skeptic's Near-Death Experience," *Skeptical Inquirer*, Summer 1994.
Terry Mattingly	"Brilliant Orbs and 'God Lite,'" *Moody*, January 1995.
Jonathan Rosen	"Rewriting the End: Elisabeth Kübler-Ross," *New York Times Magazine*, January 22, 1995.
Loyal Rue	"How Shall I Think About Death?" *Humanist*, July/August 1995.
Matthew Scully	"The Light Brigade," *National Review*, September 12, 1994.
Richard Selzer	"Raising the Dead," *Discover*, February 1994.
Andrew Stuttaford	"Frozen Future," *National Review*, September 2, 1996.
James M. Wall	"Melancholy Days," *Christian Century*, October 19, 1994.

FOR FURTHER DISCUSSION

CHAPTER 1

1. William E. Phipps argues that patients in a permanent vegetative state (PVS) are incapable of conscious thought and are therefore dead. In Phipps's opinion, why are PVS patients incapable of conscious thought? What evidence does Jim Holt present to support his contention that comatose patients are capable of some conscious thought? In your opinion, is this evidence applicable to PVS patients? Why or why not?

2. Nancy Harvey asserts that dying patients should always be provided nutritional life support. According to Anne E. Fade, how might such life support measures cause discomfort to the dying patient? Why, in her opinion, should nutrition and hydration be withheld unless the dying patient requests it? Which author's arguments do you find more persuasive? Explain.

CHAPTER 2

1. According to Ronald Dworkin, the U.S. Constitution does not prevent physicians from assisting terminally ill patients to commit suicide. In Dworkin's opinion, how can the Roe v. Wade decision be extended to legalize physician-assisted suicide? Why is the Roe v. Wade decision not applicable to assisted suicide, according to Jeffrey Rosen? Do you agree or disagree that terminally ill patients should have the legal right to commit suicide with the help of a physician? Defend your answer, using examples from the viewpoints.

2. William H.A. Carr advocates legalization of physician-assisted suicide. According to Carr, in what ways are doctors already acting to hasten the deaths of some patients? What does Louis Vernacchio say is the difference between a doctor allowing a terminally ill patient to die and participating in physician-assisted suicide? In your opinion, is it ethical for physicians to help dying patients commit suicide? Cite the viewpoints to support your answer.

CHAPTER 3

1. Thomas Lynch states that the purpose of funerals is to remind survivors of their mortality. In his view, how does this increase respect for life? What do you think David S. Toolan would say is the purpose of a funeral? In his opinion, why is an Irish-style wake appropriate only for certain people? Which type of funeral do you think is more likely to increase respect for life? Explain.

2. Ellen Uzelac contends that public displays of mourning are innovative ways for people to deal with grief. According to Michael Ventura, what is the danger in public mourning for grieving individuals? Why have such public displays become so prevalent in recent decades, in his opinion? Do you agree or disagree with Ventura's assessment? Why or why not?

CHAPTER 4

1. Kimberly Clark Sharp maintains that near-death experiences are evidence that death is not the end of life. In the views of Hayden Ebbern, Sean Mulligan, and Barry L. Beyerstein, why are such experiences unreliable as proof of an afterlife? What agenda would they say Sharp is promoting? In your opinion, do Ebbern, Mulligan, and Beyerstein believe or disbelieve in the existence of an afterlife? Cite the viewpoint to support your argument.

2. The Alcor Life Extension Foundation maintains that there is a good chance that cryonically frozen persons can be returned to life and health in the future. According to Phil Bagnall, why is it impossible to revive a frozen body? How do you think Alcor would respond to his criticisms? Give examples from the text to defend your answer.

ORGANIZATIONS TO CONTACT

The editors have compiled the following list of organizations concerned with the issues debated in this book. The descriptions are derived from materials provided by the organizations. All have publications or information available for interested readers. The list was compiled on the date of publication of the present volume; names, addresses, phone and fax numbers, and e-mail and Internet addresses may change. Be aware that many organizations may take several weeks or longer to respond to inquiries, so allow as much time as possible.

Alcor Life Extension Foundation (ALEF)
7895 E. Acoma Dr., Suite 110, Scottsdale, AZ 85260
(602) 922-9013 • (800) 367-2228
e-mail: info@alcor.org

Founded in 1972, ALEF is a group of individuals who have arranged to be cryonically suspended following their deaths. Cryonics is the process of preserving clinically dead people at ultra-low temperatures in hopes of returning them to life when medicine has become more sophisticated. ALEF's objective is to extend indefinitely the lives of its members. It currently has thirty-two members in suspension, maintained in liquid nitrogen. ALEF also conducts cryobiological research and maintains a speakers bureau. It publishes the newsletter *Alcor Phoenix* eight times a year, the quarterly magazine *Cryonics*, and several brochures and booklets.

Choice in Dying
200 Varick St., New York, NY 10014-4810
(212) 366-5540 • (800) 989-WILL • fax: (212) 366-5337
e-mail: cid@choices.org • Internet: http://www.echonyc.com

Choice in Dying educates professionals and the public on the legal, ethical, and psychological consequences of decisions concerning the terminally ill. For example, it provides physicians with information about the consequences of assisting in a patient's suicide or taking part in euthanasia. It publishes the quarterly newsletter *Choices* and the Question & Answer Series, which includes the titles *You and Your Choices*, *Advance Directives*, *Advance Directives and End-of-Life Decisions*, and *Dying at Home*.

Compassion in Dying
PO Box 75295, Seattle, WA 98125-0295
(206) 624-2775 • fax (206) 624-2673

Compassion in Dying provides information, counseling, and emotional support to terminally ill patients and their families, including information and counseling about intensive pain management, comfort or hospice care, and death-hastening methods. Its members believe that terminally ill patients who seek to hasten their deaths should not have to die alone because their friends and families fear they will be prosecuted if present. Compassion in Dying does not promote suicide but sees hastening death as a last resort when all other possibilities have been exhausted and when suffering is intolerable. It publishes several pamphlets on intensive pain management and on coping with the death of a loved one.

Death with Dignity Education Center (DDEC)

520 S. El Camino Real, Suite 710, San Mateo, CA 94402
(415) DIGNITY (344-6489) • fax: (415) 344-8100
e-mail: ddec@aol.com

The DDEC promotes a comprehensive, humane, responsive system of care for terminally ill patients. Its members believe that a dying patient's choices should be given the utmost respect and consideration. The center serves as an information resource for the public and the media and promotes strategies for advancing a responsive system of care for terminally ill patients on educational, legal, legislative, and public-policy fronts. The DDEC publishes several fact sheets, including *Misconceptions in the Debate on Death with Dignity, The Situation in Florida, Dying in the U.S.A.: A Call for Public Debate*, and *The Issue: From the Individual's Perspective*, all of which are available in an information package by request.

Euthanasia Research and Guidance Organization (ERGO)

24829 Norris Ln., Junction City, OR 97448-9559
phone and fax: (541) 998-1873
e-mail: ergo@efn.org • Internet: http://www.finalexit.org

ERGO works to achieve the passage of laws permitting physician-assisted suicide for the advanced terminally ill and the irreversibly ill who are suffering unbearably. It seeks to accomplish its goals by providing research data, addressing the public through the media, and helping raise campaign funds. It also helps patients to die by supplying drug information, technique advice, and moral support via e-mail or postal mail or through the manual *Final Exit*.

Funeral & Memorial Societies of America (FAMSA)

PO Box 10, Hinesburg, VT 05461
(802) 482-3437 • fax: (802) 482-2879
e-mail: famsa@funerals.org • Internet: http://www.funerals.org/famsa

Funeral & Memorial Societies of America works to promote the affordability, dignity, and simplicity of funeral rites and memorial services. It strives to provide every person with the opportunity to predetermine the type of funeral or memorial service he or she desires. It provides information on body and organ donation and on funeral costs, and it lobbies for reform of funeral regulations at the state and federal levels. It publishes the *FAMSA—Directory of Member Societies* periodically, the quarterly newsletter the *Leader*, and other information.

Hastings Center

255 Elm Rd., Briarcliff Manor, NY 10510

(914) 762-8500 • fax: (914) 762-2124

Since its founding in 1969, the center has played a central role in responding to advances in the medical, biological, and social sciences by raising ethical questions related to such advances. It conducts research and provides consultations on ethical issues such as assisted suicide and offers a forum for exploration and debate. The center publishes books, papers, guidelines, and the bimonthly *Hastings Center Report*.

Hemlock Society

PO Box 101810, Denver, CO 80250

(303) 639-1202 • (800) 247-7421 • fax (303) 639-1224

e-mail: hemlock@privatei.com

Internet: http://www.hemlock.org/hemlock

The society believes that terminally ill individuals have the right to commit suicide. It supports the practice of voluntary suicide and physician-assisted suicide for the terminally ill. The society publishes books on suicide, death and dying—including *Final Exit*, a guide to those who are suffering with terminal illnesses and considering suicide—and the *Hemlock Quarterly*.

Human Life International (HLI)

7845 Airpark Rd., Suite E, Gaithersburg, MD 20879

(301) 670-7884

HLI is a pro-life education and research organization that believes that the fetus is human from the moment of conception. It offers positive alternatives to abortion, assisted suicide, and euthanasia. The organization publishes *Confessions of a ProLife Missionary*, *Deceiving Birth Controllers*, and the monthly newsletters *HLI Reports* and *PRI Review*.

International Anti-Euthanasia Task Force (IAETF)

PO Box 760, Steubenville, OH 43952

(614) 282-3810

The IAETF is a group of individuals who oppose euthanasia. The group works to provide information on euthanasia and related end-of-life issues, to promote the right of all persons to be treated with respect, dignity, and compassion, and to combat attitudes, programs, and policies that its members believe threaten the lives of those who are medically vulnerable. It conducts seminars and workshops and publishes the bimonthly newsletter *IAETF Update*.

International Association for Near-Death Studies (IANDS)

PO Box 502, East Windsor Hill, CT 06028

(860) 528-5144 • fax: (860) 528-9169

Internet: http://www.iands.org/iands

IANDS is a worldwide organization of scientists, scholars, and others who are interested in or who have had near-death experiences. It supports the scientific study of near-death experiences and their implications, fosters communication among researchers on this topic, and sponsors support groups in which people can discuss their near-death experiences. The association publishes the quarterly newsletter *Vital Signs*.

National Hospice Organization (NHO)

1901 N. Moore St., Suite 901, Arlington, VA 22209
(703) 243-5900 • (800) 658-8898 • fax: (703) 525-5762

The NHO opposes euthanasia and assisted suicide. It works to educate the public about the benefits of hospice care for the terminally ill and their families. It promotes the idea that, with the proper care and pain medication, the terminally ill can live out their lives comfortably and in the company of their families. It publishes the quarterlies *Hospice Journal* and *Hospice Magazine*, the annual *Guide to the Nation's Hospices*, the *Hospice Fact Sheet*, and a variety of books and monographs.

BIBLIOGRAPHY OF BOOKS

Johann C. Arnold
I Tell You a Mystery: Life, Death, and Eternity. Farmington, PA: Plough Publishing House, 1997.

Margaret P. Battin
The Least Worst Death: Essays in Bioethics on the End of Life. New York: Oxford University Press, 1994.

Margaret P. Battin and Arthur G. Lipman, eds.
Drug Use in Assisted Suicide and Euthanasia. New York: Pharmaceutical Products Press, 1996.

Lucy Bregman and Sara Thiermann
First Person Mortal: Personal Narratives of Dying, Death, and Grief. New York: Paragon House, 1995.

Daniel Callahan
The Troubled Dream of Life: Living with Mortality. New York: Simon & Schuster, 1993.

Mally Cox-Chapman
The Case for Heaven: Near-Death Experiences as Evidence of the Afterlife. New York: Putnam, 1995.

Lynne Ann DeSpelder and Albert Lee Strickland, eds.
The Path Ahead: Readings in Death and Dying. Mountain View, CA: Mayfield Publishing, 1995.

Ronald Dworkin
Life's Dominion: An Argument About Abortion, Euthanasia, and Individual Freedom. New York: Knopf, 1993.

Sally Friedman
Swimming the Channel. New York: Farrar, Straus, and Giroux, 1996.

Gere B. Fulton and Eileen K. Metress
Perspectives on Death and Dying. Boston, MA: Jones and Bartlett, 1995.

Robert J. Geis
Personal Existence After Death: Reductionist Circularities and the Evidence. Peru, IL: Sherwood Sugden, 1995.

Earl A. Grollman, ed.
Bereaved Children and Teens: A Support Guide for Parents and Professionals. Boston: Beacon Press, 1995.

Herbert Hendin
Seduced by Death: Doctors, Patients, and the Dutch Cure. New York: Norton, 1997.

James M. Hoefler and Brian E. Kamoie
Deathright: Culture, Medicine, Politics, and the Right to Die. Boulder, CO: Westview Press, 1994.

Marylou Hughes
Bereavement and Support: Healing in a Group Environment. Washington, DC: Taylor & Francis, 1995.

Stephen Jamison
Final Acts of Love: Families, Friends, and Assisted Dying. New York: Putnam, 1995.

Robert A. Jonas
Rebecca: A Father's Journey from Grief to Gratitude. New York: Crossroad, 1996.

Mary Jones
Love After Death: Counseling in Bereavement. Bristol, PA: J. Kingsley, 1995.

Karen Katafiasz
Finding Your Way Through Grief. St. Meinrad, IN: Abbey Press, 1995.

Dennis Klass et al., eds.	*Continuing Bonds: New Understandings of Grief.* Washington, DC: Taylor & Francis, 1996.
Lucinda P. Knox and Michael D. Knox	*Last Wishes: A Handbook to Guide Your Survivors.* Berkeley, CA: Ulysses Press, 1994.
George S. Lair	*Counseling the Terminally Ill: Sharing the Journey.* Washington, DC: Taylor & Francis, 1996.
Barbara J. Logue	*Last Rights: Death Control and the Elderly in America.* New York: Lexington Books, 1993.
Alan Meisel	*The Right to Die,* 2nd ed. New York: Wiley Law Publications, 1995.
Jonathan D. Moreno, ed.	*Arguing Euthanasia: The Controversy over Mercy Killing, Assisted Suicide, and the "Right to Die."* New York: Simon & Schuster, 1995.
New York State Task Force on Life and the Law	*When Death Is Sought: Assisted Suicide and Euthanasia in the Medical Context.* New York: New York State Task Force on Life and the Law, 1994.
Sherwin B. Nuland	*How We Die: Reflections on Life's Final Chapter.* New York: Knopf, 1994.
Mary O'Donnell	*HIV/AIDS: Loss, Grief, Challenge, and Hope.* Washington, DC: Taylor & Francis, 1996.
Timothy E. Quill	*A Midwife Through the Dying Process: Stories of Healing and Hard Choices at the End of Life.* Baltimore: Johns Hopkins University Press, 1996.
Timothy E. Quill	*Death and Dignity: Making Choices and Taking Charge.* New York: Norton, 1993.
Jenny Randles and Peter Hough	*The Afterlife: An Investigation into the Mysteries of Life After Death.* New York: Berkeley Books, 1994.
Richard Selzer	*Raising the Dead.* New York: Whittle Books, in association with Viking Penguin, 1994.
Peter Singer	*Rethinking Life and Death: The Collapse of Our Traditional Ethics.* New York: St. Martin's Press, 1995.
Ganga Stone	*Start the Conversation: The Book About Death You Were Hoping to Find.* New York: Warner Books, 1996.
David C. Treadway	*Dead Reckoning: A Therapist Confronts His Own Grief.* New York: BasicBooks, 1996.
Michael Ventura	*The Death of Frank Sinatra: A Novel.* New York: Henry Holt, 1996.
Charlie Walton	*Packing for the Big Trip: Life Benefits from Death Awareness.* Ventura, CA: Pathfinder Publications, 1997.
Robert F. Weir	*Physician-Assisted Suicide.* Bloomington: Indiana University Press, 1997.
James L. Werth Jr.	*Rational Suicide? Implications for Mental Health Professionals.* Washington, DC: Taylor & Francis, 1996.

INDEX

actions during, 28, 29, 51
cessation of nutrition for, 39, 45, 51
lack of suffering in, 20
life support for those in, 26
longevity of those in, 19, 21, 28, 29
misdiagnosed, 32
numbers of persons in, 25, 29
and quality of life, 49
reasons for, 29
reversible, 33
see also comatose patients
Phipps, William E., 17
physician-assisted death. *See under* death
physicians
    and do-not-resuscitate order, 61
    and end-of-life treatment, 41-42, 47,
        51, 85-86
    and life-sustaining measures, 60
    opinions on assisted death, 76-77,
        81, 93
Planned Parenthood v. Casey, 57, 59, 67, 68
Pohl, Melvin I., 117
Posner, Richard, 71
powers of attorney
    for health care, 25, 41, 61, 88-90
    see also advance directives; living wills
President's Commission for the Study of
    Ethical Problems in Medicine, 31
"Prolongation of Life" (Pope Pius XII),
    30

quality of life
    and advance directives, 92
    and brain death, 23
    for disabled, 50-51, 92-93
    for terminally ill, 43, 50, 85
Quill, Timothy E., 62, 63, 76
Quill v. Vacco, 60, 78, 81
Quindlen, Anna, 74
Quinlan, Karen, 19-20, 29, 31, 60, 61,
    68

Rando, Therese A., 116, 118, 120
Rawlings, Maurice, 158, 161
Recollections of Death (Sabom), 157
Redefining Death (Gervais), 22
Redgrave, Lynn, 100
Rehnquist, William, 66
Reinhardt, Stephen, 59, 66-71
religion
    and afterlife, 156-61, 165-67
    in America, 157, 158, 159
    Catholic Church, on death, 30
    on double effect, 82-83
    on euthanasia, 76, 83-84
    on life-support systems, 40-42, 84
    and mourning, 120
    and near-death experiences, 155-62

resurgence in, 166
of the resuscitated, 158-59, 162
on suicide, 75-76
right to die
    advance directives protect, 87-90
    Constitution protects, 56-63
    con, 64-72
    and terminally ill, 57-63
right to live, advance directives may not
    protect, 91-95
Ring, Kenneth, 157-59, 161
Roe v. Wade, 57, 65, 67
Rogers, David, 77
Romano, Darla, 102, 104
Rosen, Jeffrey, 64
Rothstein, Barbara, 57, 58

Sabom, Michael, 157
Sanders, Catherine, 116, 118
Saved by the Light (Brinkley), 158
Schneiderman, Laurence J., 29
Schopenhauer, Arthur, 32
Serdahely, William J., 151
Shadowlands (movie), 100
Shakespeare for My Father (Redgrave), 100
Sharp, Kimberly Clark, 149
slippery-slope argument, 23, 58-59,
    69, 75, 84-85
Society for Psychical Research, 165
Solomon, Andrew, 65
soul, 18, 164-66
Spiro, Guy, 149
Stuttaford, Andrew, 175
suicide
    assisted, 57-63, 65-66, 69-71, 77-78,
        81
    and grief, 118, 120
    religion on, 75-76
    see also death, physician-assisted;
        euthanasia
Sullivan, Robert, 39
Sunny von Bulow Coma and Brain
    Trauma Foundation, 29
SUPPORT study, 85
Surviving Grief and Learning to Live Again
    (Sanders), 116

Taxel, Laura, 87
"Tears in Heaven" (Clapton), 100
technology
    changes experience of death, 109
    for physical comfort, 47
    prolonging death by, 45-49, 74-75,
        92
terminally ill
    caring for, 50, 110, 111-12, 119, 153
    easing pain of, 48, 82
    families of, 37, 40-42, 46, 110